I0625267

THE FOUR HORSEMEN

CLASHES OF THE CALIPHATE I

THE FOUR HORSEMEN

C. M. Amos

The Four Horsemen
Copyright 2024 C.M. Amos

All rights reserved. No part of this book may be reproduced or transmitted in any form or by any means, electronic or mechanical, including photocopying and recording, or by any information storage and retrieval system, without permission in writing from the publisher.

All Scripture quotations are taken from the King James Version, public domain.

ISBN (paperback): 979-8-218-46630-5

Disclaimer

I do not claim to be an expert in history or that every detail in this book has 100% accuracy. History has many perspectives, and sources do not always agree on the facts. This book is intended to give you a general understanding of history, not a precise one. Concerning my sources, I tried to list sources that are easily accessible to every reader and do not require the purchases of any books. Because of this, some sources may be deleted over time, especially YouTube videos, but if you search, you can find alternate sources containing the same information.

Contents

Preface

The horrifying events that have been unfolding over the last few decades paled in comparison to what I was now watching. Many of us knew that something biblical was taking place, but no one seemed to be able to find the words to explain it. Watching hundreds of videos that tried to tie these events to Bible prophecy left me with more questions than answers. These questions demanded answers that didn't require mental gymnastics to be able to understand. I needed to understand, not only for myself, but for my children and grandchildren. What I am about to describe is graphic and morbidly violent. Reader discretion is advised.

In April 2013, the world watched an extremist Islamic group called ISIS (Islamic State of Iraq and Syria), now called ISIL (Islamic State of Iraq and the Levant), release an onslaught of violent videos that would continue for exactly forty-two months, as they fought to reestablish an Islamic caliphate in Iraq, Syria, and Libya. These videos depicted executions, beheadings, and crucifixions, along with many other heinous acts against whom they considered to be infidels according to Islam. Adults and children were shown buried up to their necks in the hot desert sand as the sun beat down on them. Severed heads were prominently displayed in rows on fence posts while small children were ordered to kick other severed heads around in the sand. Images of bloodied bodies of women were shown stacked in piles in various places, and reports of them feeding their soldiers alive to dogs began to surface.

Everything I had learned about what the Great Tribulation would look like, and how long it would last, seemed to be unfolding before my eyes.

And I looked, and behold a pale horse:
and his name that sat on him was Death, and Hell followed with him.
And power was given unto them over a fourth part of the earth,
to kill with sword, and with hunger, and with death,
and with the beasts of the earth.
Revelation 6:8 KJV

Granted, it wasn't a fourth of the actual earth, but it was about a fourth of the Middle East. Was this a foreshadow of things to come or had the Tribulation started? I began searching feverishly through history and Bible prophecies for six hours every night after work for the next five to six years for the answer. Over time, the confusion I had about the Book of Revelation began lifting like a dense fog, and things that once puzzled me now seemed crystal clear. I'll never forget the excitement I felt as all the dots began connecting. Only one question remained unanswered. How is it that the Church overlooked all these events in history that had clearly depicted the four horsemen of Revelation?

Neither do men light a candle and put it
under a bushel, but on a candlestick;
and it giveth light unto all that are in the house.
Matthew 5:15 KJV

My instructions were clear. I had to share what I found with anyone who was willing to listen, or in this case, read.

Additional Sources

"New ISIS video shows execution of 21 Christians." CBS Evening News. Live on February 15, 2015. YouTube video. 1:47. https://youtu.be/eX172j6U _KI?si=_kSkf_faLh-CjkgJ

"IS Teaches Children How to do Beheadings." Associated Press. Live on July 19, 2015. YouTube video. 1:50. https://youtu.be/AG7Ct0EqTFI

Spark, Joseph. Atrocities Committed by ISIS in Syria & Iraq: ISIL/Islamic State/Daesh. eBook. Conceptual Kings, 2014.

Newton, Jennifer. Daily Mail. "ISIS commanders are fed alive to DOGS for failing their duties in brutal new form of execution aimed at ending the group's run of military defeats." May 23, 2016. Accessed January 8, 2024. https://www.dailymail.co.uk/news/article-3604501/ISIS-commanders -fed-alive-DOCS-failing-duties-brutal-new-form-execution-aimed -ending-group-s-run-military-defeats.html

Introduction

The Book of Revelation is full of mystical creatures like frogs, horse-human shaped locusts, beasts, horsemen, kings ruled by a dragon, angels, and others who all appear to be fighting for global domination centering around "a Great Sea" or what I believe to be the Mediterranean Sea. Most of us love a good sci-fi/mystery/thriller, and the Book of Revelation reads like a mix of Alfred Hitchcock, Game of Thrones, Star Trek, and The Hunger Games all rolled into one.

The prophecy in Revelation is God's last known written word to mankind and stands as the greatest unsolved mystery ever written. It can be found as the last book of the Holy Bible, given by God, to warn his people of events to come that will escalate until the end of all things, as we know them to be.

The Four Horsemen will take you on a journey that bypasses the first five chapters of Revelation, which deserve a book of their own, and begins with the first eight verses of the sixth chapter, where this action packed, sci-fi-like mystery seems to begin and appears to have been unfolding for the last 1,000 years. Revelation 6 is where the mysterious four horsemen begin their ride and you begin what may well be one of the most important journeys you will ever take in your lifetime.

My hope is that as you watch these events unfold in history and the identity of the Four Horsemen become self-evident, it will be as exciting for you as it was for me. The Four Horsemen is the first book of a series called "Clashes of the Caliphate," detailing all the forces at work in the greatest mystery ever written, the Book of Revelation. This series will cause you to question everything you think you know about the Tribulation, the rapture, the beasts of Revelation, the ten kings, and the image in the book of Daniel. It will also bring simple clarity to things that have confused you. These things have been sealed and hidden from our understanding until the time of the end, and that time is now.

And he said, Go thy way, Daniel:
for the words are closed up and sealed till
the time of the end.
Daniel 12:9

Notes

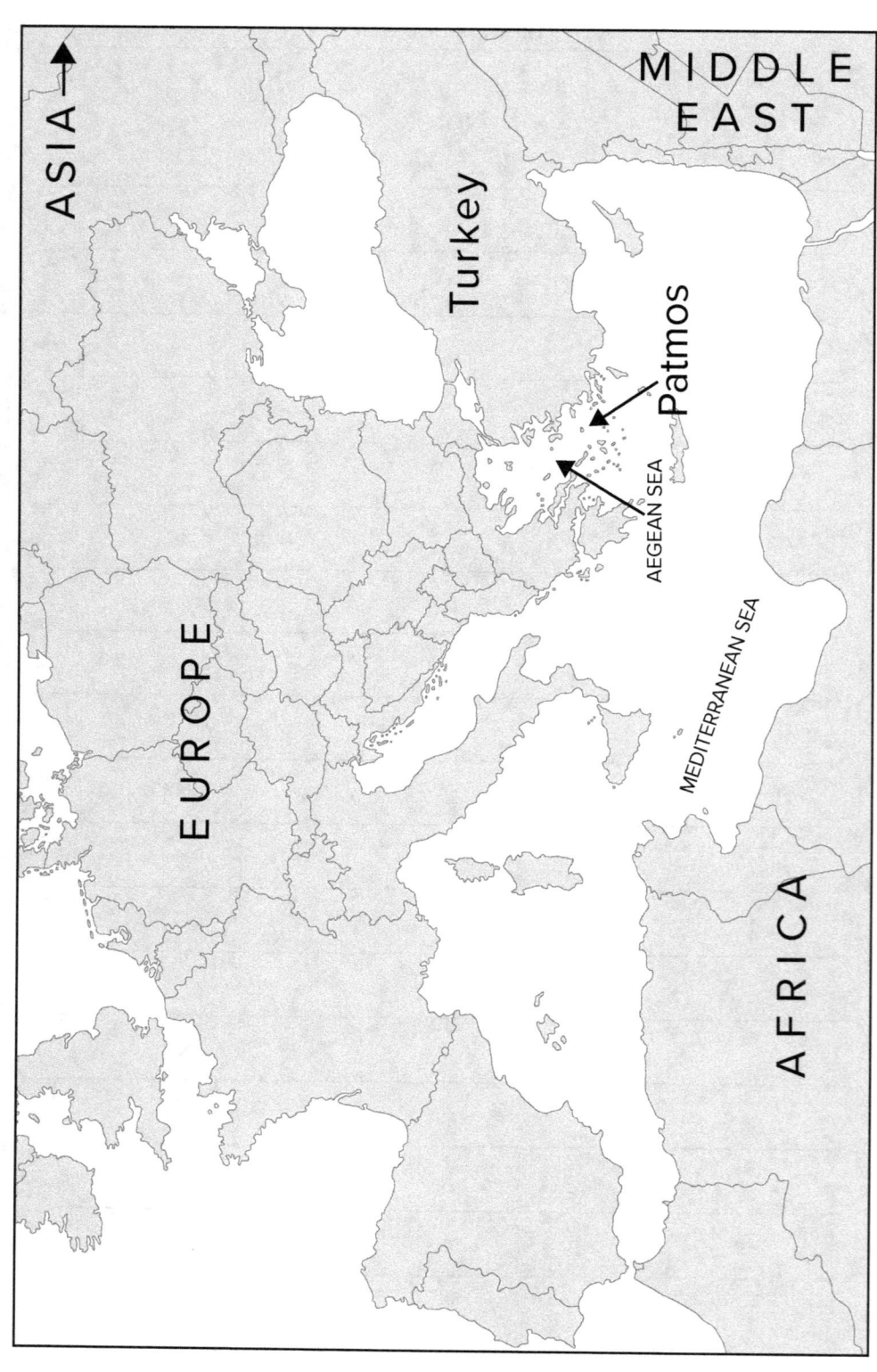

Chapter 1

From Sea to Shining Key

The vast expanse of lands that cradle the "Great" Mediterranean Sea have played host to seven of the most powerful empires in recorded history, from Ancient Babylon to the Ottoman Empire. He who ruled those lands also ruled the sea along with its many resources and trade routes linking the continents of Asia, Africa, and Europe. The Mediterranean islands also played many vital roles, including hosting fortresses, cities, cash crops, and prisons. One of those prisons was located on the island of Patmos in the Aegean Sea, the northeastern arm of the Mediterranean between Turkey and Greece.

Imagine that we are taking a ferry from the coast of Greece to the island of Patmos. The journey would be a fifty-six-mile trip that would take seven to twelve hours to complete. As our ferry approaches the small, remote island, what appears to be a fortress emerges on the horizon. Numerous small, white buildings shore up the fortress and look as if they are being guarded by the steep, jagged cliffs surrounding them. This fortress and conglomeration of small white buildings is the St. John Monastery, built by monks in AD 1088 over what is known as "The Cave of the Apocalypse." The monastery has three hundred rooms and houses the forty monks who tend to it. The fortress has forty-foot- to fifty-foot-high walls and sports a large bell on top that was sounded by the monks of years gone by to warn of approaching pirates. The monks have faithfully guarded, defended, and promoted this cave for almost one thousand years while expanding the monastery.

Stepping down from the monastery and into the twenty-one-foot by twenty-four-foot cave, a door peers outside with a spectacular view of waves crashing against the large and treacherous rocks that line a small cove just outside the cave. (This is where a man named John went in and out while serving his sentence of hard labor.) The cave is dimly lit by three fissures in the ceiling whose light from above seems to showcase a rock where it is believed John laid his head and gazed into the heavens as he watched a vision of mysterious and bizarre creatures, beasts, and a dragon contend for global domination—until their ultimate defeat.

This man named John is known as St. John the Divine, St. John the Theologian, John the Revelator, and the "disciple that Jesus loved" because he always seemed to be able to see and hear the heart behind the words that Jesus taught. John had been exiled to Patmos by the Roman Emperor Domitian for preaching the gospel of Jesus around AD 70–95. Patmos is now part of Greece but, in John's day, it was part of Rome and was used for exiled prisoners due to its remoteness and steep, jagged cliffs and rocks. Today, it stands as a World Heritage Site, designated by the United Nations Educational, Scientific and Cultural Organization (UNESCO).

John's faithful follower, Prosphorus, likely listened to, wrote, and delivered John's vision to the church in Ephesus, one of the seven churches in Asia (known today as Turkey). This vision would survive a fifteen-hundred-year journey from the cave to Ephesus, through wars, famines, regime changes, and ethnic cleansings to be scrutinized by kings and councils and become the last book of the Holy Bible called the Book of Revelation.

It is nothing short of a miracle that the monastery, cave, and vision have survived intact to this day. The monastery thrives as a high-traffic tourist destination, and the Book of Revelation lives on as one of the most important, highly contested, and mysterious books of the Holy Bible. For nearly

The St. John Monastery was built by monks in AD 1088 over what is known as "The Cave of the Apocalypse."

The view from inside the Cave of the Apocalypse. John likely had this same view during his exile.

two thousand years, the Church has struggled to unlock the multitude of mysteries contained in John's vision describing the apocalyptic events that will ultimately lead to the end of the world as we know it.

While John lay gazing into the heavens through the fissures, perhaps hoping for some rest from his sentence of hard labor while imagining the day he would be reunited with Jesus and meditating on his teachings, he receives an epic vision of a majestic and spectacular being sitting on a throne holding a Pandora's book containing the fate of humanity and sealed with seven seals. The throne sits on a sea of crystal overshadowed by an emerald rainbow and is surrounded by twenty-four elders and four unimaginable and terrifying beasts. John is so overwhelmed by what he is seeing at one point that he rolls to his face and becomes completely unresponsive. Stark warnings to the seven churches in Asia are pronounced as lightning, thunder, and trumpets permeate the atmosphere. During this ominous scene, John hears one of the four beasts standing by the throne say, "Come and see." The first seal of the Pandora's book is opened, and John watches a man with a bow in his hand riding a white horse leap from its pages into the earth on a mission to conquer it.

The first questions that demand answers are what is this horse, why is it white, who is this man, and when is this to take place? We are given a clue in the first verse of Revelation where it states these things would "shortly come to pass," but what does that mean exactly? To find the key that helps unlock the answer to these questions, we need to leave our ferry, travel back in time to around 500 to 600 BC, and visit Ancient Babylon, located in modern day Iraq. There, we will listen to a man named Daniel, who had a similar vision that was interpreted by the Angel Gabriel.

In Daniel 8, Daniel shares a vision he had about a goat attacking a ram. The Angel Gabriel explains to Daniel that these animals represent countries or kingdoms that would fight against each other for global domination in the future. Since there is no valid reason to believe that a horse would be interpreted any differently than the ram or goat, it would stand to reason that a horse is also a kingdom or country that will shortly arise and fight for global domination. We now understand the White Horse is a kingdom or country that will shortly contend for global domination, and we can take a seat in the arena of world history. There we will watch as Rome, the greatest Mediterranean empire of John's day, falls and the next great Mediterranean empire arises from the "Great Sea." History itself will solve this great mystery, and the interpretation of the four horsemen will become self-evident as we zoom in on events that took place during the last two thousand years.

Nations align
While others collide
A storm approaches
Nowhere to hide
Voices trumpet
Behind every hill
A faint voice cries out
Hold your peace and be still

Additional Sources

"Canonicity and Acceptance of Revelation (in Revelation)." Anabaptistwiki. https://anabaptistwiki.org/mediawiki/index.php?title=Canonicity_and _Acceptance_of_Revelation_%28in_Revelation%29.

"John 13:23 - Jesus Predicts His Betrayal." Bible Hub. https://biblehub.com /john/13-23.htm.

Kruger, Michael. "The Book of Revelation: How Difficult Was Its Journey into the Canon?" Canon Fodder, April 14, 2023. https://www.michae ljkruger.com/the-book-of-revelation-how-difficult-was-its-journey-into -the-canon/.

"Patmos Island. Seven Churches of Revelation Tour." YouTube, June 10, 2017. https://www.youtube.com/watch?v=VnF9tHGYoQ0.

"St. John the Apostle." Encyclopaedia Britannica, March 15, 2024. https:// www.britannica.com/biography/Saint-John-the-Apostle.

"Who was John the Revelator?" Adapted from Robert Q. Bailey, "John, the Man," Illustrated Bible Life, MAM 1997, WordAction Publishing Company™. https://www.barefootonline.com/vcmedia/2420/2420495.pdf.

Chapter 2

Oh Say, Can You Sea?

Up until his exile, John had watched Rome rise to its zenith of power, much like many of us have watched America rise to its zenith of power. In AD 117, shortly after John's exile and release, Trajan began his rule, and Rome encompassed the lands around the entire Mediterranean, including half of the Black Sea and part of the Red Sea. The burden of overseeing such a massive territory became too great for a single monarch to bear. As a result, the empire was divided into East and West Rome, two rulers were appointed, and two armies were formed. In AD 330, the name of its capital Byzantium was changed to Constantinople, and after the Renaissance, divided Rome became known as the Byzantine Empire.

Rome's capital of Constantinople is now known as Istanbul and is located in Turkey on the Bosphorus Strait that connects the Black Sea to the Marmara Sea. The Marmara Sea connects to the Aegean Sea, where John received his vision. The Aegean Sea connects to the Mediterranean Sea, which is the center point of the Indian, Atlantic, and Arctic Oceans. The Bosphorus Strait was and is extremely important for worldwide shipping as well as defense. This makes Turkey as important today as Asia was in John's day. Is it any wonder that John was told in Revelation 2:13 that Satan, himself, chose this area as his dwelling place? East Rome, who had jurisdiction over this strait, was always richer and would survive West Rome by nearly one thousand years.

Various books list over two hundred reasons why Rome fell, but those reasons are lodged around three major waves of woe that hit Rome. The first woe started in AD 376 when Atilla the Hun began his campaigns in the lands lying to the northeast of Rome. These attacks drove numerous "barbarian" tribes into the western half of the empire to seek refuge, and they colonized large territories within Rome's borders. It's much like what we have watched happen in America and countless other countries. As wars break out and Islamic groups, like ISIS and Hamas, terrorize the Middle East, countless refugees are driven out of those areas into the rest of the world. West Rome was no more successful at dispelling or integrating these colonies of people groups than we have been. Even here in America, we have Muslims colonizing and setting up their own territories while subjecting or trying to subject these territories to Sharia law. Another example of colonization in America is Chinatown. China has also set up its own police stations in at least seven cities in the US to monitor and arrest its own citizens who currently reside in the US.

One of the people groups who fled from the forces of Atilla the Hun and colonized within Rome's northwestern borders were the Germanics. Odoacer, the king of the Germanics, dealt the final blow to West Rome, deposing the last of the Western Roman Emperors, Romulus Augustulus. Centralized power was never regained in West Rome, and over time, it localized in East Rome. The reach of Rome remained in the West but continued to be weakened until it completely dissipated and was replaced by the territories claimed by these "barbarian" tribes. These groups included the Vandals, Suebs, Visigoths, Franks, Lombards, Gepids, Burgundians, Slavs (Huns), and the Ostrogoths, all who eventually developed their own nation states that completely replaced West Rome. Some of them survived and grew to become the countries we know today along the Mediterranean. For example, the Franks became France, the Germanic tribes became Germany, and so on.

The dark shaded area is the majoirty of the Roman Empire at its height. The dotted line indicates the approximate division between East and West Rome.

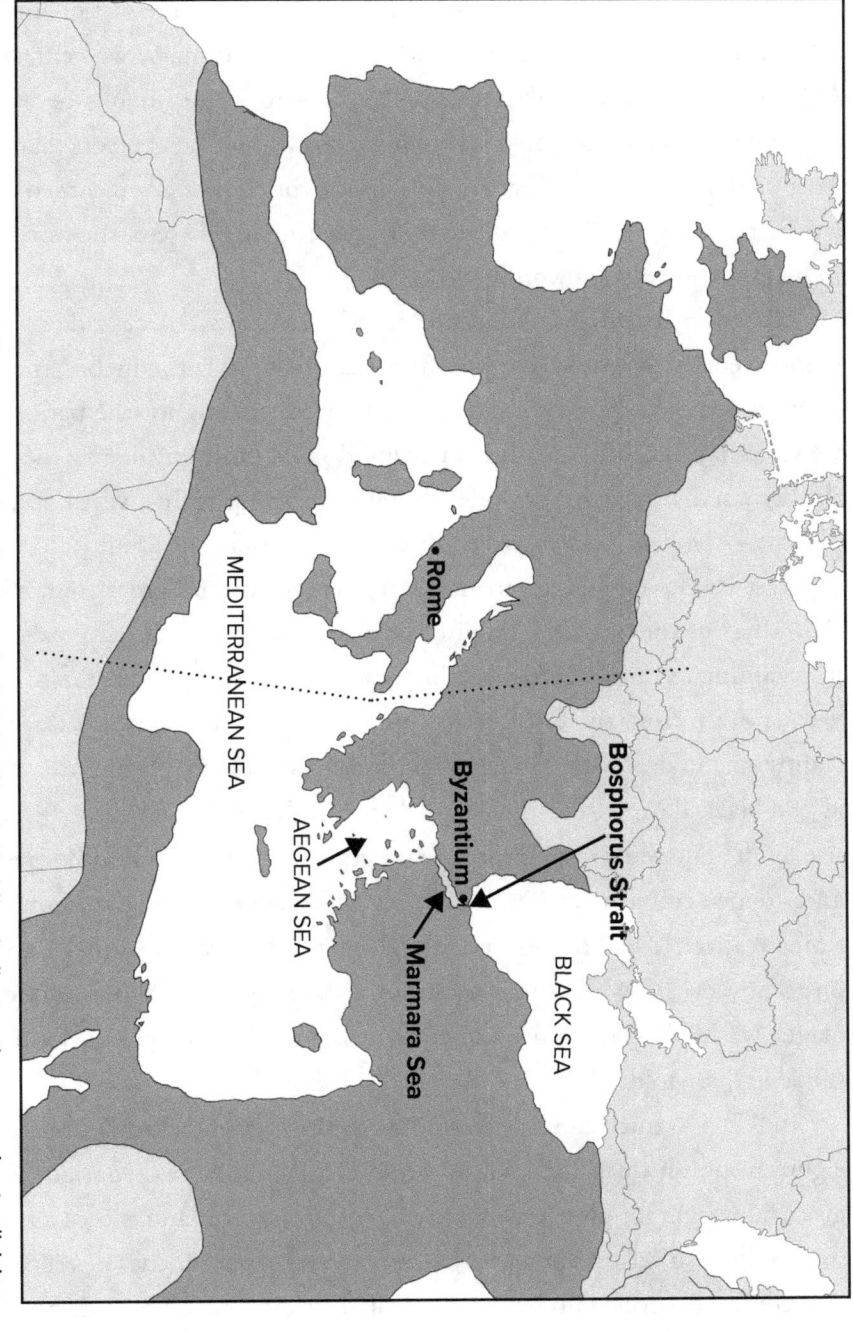

Later, the Bosphorus Strait, that had made East Rome so rich and powerful, became the avenue through which the second major woe entered. In AD 535, an event took place that's likely not in history books because it's only recently been discovered through science with advancements that didn't exist at that time. The effects of this apocalyptic event are recorded in the writings of kings, scribes, and emperors. Starting in AD 536, the worst years in history are recorded worldwide.

Whatever it was that happened in AD 535 caused a cascade of apocalyptic events that would last over fifty years. This event launched the Dark Ages, wiped out entire civilizations, and paved the way for the nations that we see today. Science now shows us why Rome's most formidable foe wasn't the barbarians, Persians, or the Arabs but something against which it had no defense—the flea. And it entered through the Bosphorus Strait.

East Rome had been warring to protect its eastern border from the Persian kings of the Sassanid Empire (Iran today), while making great strides in regaining territories it had lost in West Rome. During the battle to retake Verona, Italy, from the Ostrogoths, Justinian's army was called back to Constantinople to deal with a much larger foe—the bubonic plague, also known as the black death. Records tell us that East Rome buried, threw into the sea, built into walls, or put into mass graves ten thousand bodies per day and stopped counting at 250,000. When this plague entered Constantinople, Rome realized it had overextended itself once again and was unable to hold on to any of the West Rome territories it had regained. What caused this plague was biblical in nature and created climate chaos that made food more valuable than gold.

In AD 536 thick clouds covering the entire earth blocked out the sun for eighteen months, causing a two-year winter. The sun was reported to have given faint light for only four hours a day, and the farmland was covered in a thick yellowish dust. China and Japan recorded several inches of yellow dust that could be scooped up by the handful. This dust, blood rain, or no rain at all along with a lack of sunlight created droughts that caused worldwide famines and wiped out entire civilizations. In England, half the people in the villages were dead, and the oceans, trees, and lands weren't producing. This era not only gave us great movies, like Robin Hood, but marked the beginning of the Dark Ages, indeed. But what had caused the sun to be darkened and was this a sign from God that the four horsemen, who John had prophesied about five hundred years earlier, were about to start their ride? Did this event mark the opening of the first seal in the Book of Revelation that would lead to the Great and Terrible Day of the Lord?

> Blow ye the trumpet in Zion and sound an
> alarm in my holy mountain: let all the inhabitants
> of the land tremble: for the Day of the Lord
> cometh, for it is nigh at hand.
> A day of darkness and gloominess, a day of
> clouds and thick darkness, as the morning
> spread upon the mountains: a great people
> and strong; there hath not been ever the like,
> neither shall be any more after it, even to
> the years of many generations.
> A fire devoureth before them; and behind them
> a flame burneth: the land is as the garden
> of Eden before them, and behind them a
> desolate wilderness; yea, and nothing
> shall escape them.
> The appearance of them is as the appearance
> of horses; and as horsemen, so shall they run.
> Joel 2:1–4

Scientists believe only three things can cause these kinds of effects—

comets, volcanoes, or asteroids. If you watch the You Tube video source link titled "536 AD The Worst Year in History," you will see that by carefully examining tree rings from all over the world, drilling down for samples from both the north and south polar ice caps, examining bones and other evidence, science has not only eliminated a comet or asteroid as the cause but has proven that it was likely caused by an eruption of the Krakatoa Volcano, located in the South China Sea between Indonesia and Asia.

But wait, what does the flea have to do with any of this? While examining evidence, it was discovered that the bubonic plague originated in Ethiopia, located near the Horn of Africa that forms the Strait of Bab-el-Mandeb, joining the Red Sea to the Indian Ocean. While examining the bodies of dead fleas in Ethiopia, scientists discovered clots in their stomachs that can only form in temperatures below twenty-five degrees, likely from the sun being blocked out for an extended period. It's believed that when famine and disease killed all the rats and other animals, the fleas began seeking humans as their host, carrying the plague from rats to humans. Rome had an insatiable lust for the ivory shipped from Ethiopia, and the ships that carried it to East Rome traveled right through the Bosphorus Strait to Constantinople and unloaded 100,000 tons of ivory every year. Oh say, can you sea?

The residents of Constantinople who weren't killed by the plague fled into other parts of the empire, causing a rampant uptick in the plague's spread. While East Rome was retreating from its war efforts to regain West Rome territories and to face this pandemonium, there were stirrings of the next empire that would soon arise and release yet another biblical and apocalyptic force that we are still facing, but on a much larger scale. Much like the flea, we have no effective defenses against it. The differences are that we know it's there, but we don't know exactly where, and they may now have not only nuclear but chemical weapons that kill on a much larger scale.

A fire devoureth before them; and behind them
a flame burneth: the land is as the

garden of Eden before them
(paradise surrounded by virgins if you die for the cause of Islam)
And behind them a
desolate wilderness, yea nothing
shall escape them.
Joel 2:3

Scores of specimens that can be used as biological or chemical weapons were reported missing from labs across the world, without explanation, along with twelve nuclear warheads, alleged to have mysteriously disappeared from Texas, most of which happened while former President Barak Obama was in office. (Note that this was also when ISIS reared its ugly head.)

- Nov 16, 2016 — Iridium 192 goes missing from Iranian lab.
- April 19, 1992 — Anthrax, Ebola, and twenty-seven other specimens go missing from Fort Detric Bio-lab.
- 2014 — Polio virus goes missing from lab in Africa.
- 2013 — Twelve nuclear warheads allegedly go missing from Texas.
- 2013 — Guanarito Virus goes missing from bio-terror lab in Texas.
- 2014 — 2,300 vials of SARS go missing from The Paris Institute in France.

This list is not all inclusive. The final major woe that would take down Rome is now on the horizon—The White Horseman.

The winds howl
lifting a cloud
thunders grow
so very loud
it peers 'ore the horizon
silhouettes still unclear
it rises, none knowing
what is far, what is near

Additional Sources

"536 AD: The Worst Year in History? | Catastrophe | Full Series | Chronicle." YouTube, May 28, 2022. https://www.youtube.com/watch?v=Ax2x0MG-0Qo.

Al-Zayabi, Fahd. "Reservations on Iran Missing Iridium-192 Leading to a 'Dirty Bomb.'" Asharq Al Awsat, November 25, 2016. https://eng-archive.aawsat.com/fahd-zayabi/world-news/reservations-iran-missing-iridium-192-leading-dirty-bomb.

Bileta, Vedran. "Medieval Roman Empire: 5 Battles That (Un)Made the Byzantine Empire." TheCollector, January 11, 2022. https://www.thecollector.com/byzantine-empire-battles/.

Bileta, Vedran. "Triumph and Tragedy: 5 Battles That Made the Eastern Roman Empire." TheCollector, January 26, 2022. https://www.thecollector.com/eastern-roman-empire-battles/.

"Broken Arrows: Nuclear Weapons Accidents." Atomic Archive. https://www.atomicarchive.com/almanac/broken-arrows/index.html.

"The Fall of the Roman Empire." ushistory.org. https://www.ushistory.org/civ/6f.asp.

"French Lab Loses SARS Vials." ABC News, April 16, 2016. https://abcnews.go.com/Health/french-lab-loses-sars-vials/story?id=23349738.

"Texas Biolab Loses Deadly Guanarito Virus." ABC News, March 25, 2013. https://abcnews.go.com/Health/galveston-texas-biolab-loses-deadly-guanarito-virus/story?id=18809363.

Wasson, Donald L. "Fall of the Western Roman Empire." World History Encyclopedia, April 30, 2023. https://www.worldhistory.org/article/835/fall-of-the-western-roman-empire/.

Chapter 3

Align in the Sand

Shortly after the eruption of AD 535, the cornerstone of the next empire, that would soon conquer Rome, was put in place by a man who is said to have been born in AD 570. His religious writings created an incubator that provided stomping grounds for the "White Horse of Revelation" to grow until it was strong enough, in numbers, to carry its first rider into a series of endless wars with a mission of global domination.

DISCLAIMER

These events cannot be verified to ever have taken place as no written or archaeological evidence supports the existence of the city of Mecca during this time or the water needed to support such a large city. Absolutely no evidence exists of anyone named Muhammad who lived or worked in this area or along the trade routes that he is claimed to have traveled during this time period. (Watch the video source link titled "Investigating Islam with Dr. Jay Smith by Calvary Chapel.") This story, based solely on Islamic sources, appears to be legend more than fact.

The volcanic eruption of AD 535 caused a famine that spread to Arabia, driving many of its warring tribes to Mecca in search of food. Mecca was the hub of (Saudi) Arabia's commerce, trade, culture, and religion. The Kaaba, in

Mecca, housed over two hundred gods that were worshipped in the region.

Abd Allah bin Al-Muttalib and his wife, Amina, rose to the challenge created by the famine and became well-known for their charity by distributing food. The rise of every empire always begins with the birth of a man, and around AD 570, they had a son that they named Muhammad, now known as the prophet of Islam. The family had earned themselves a prominent place in society and were well-known among the tribes, but family fame didn't prepare little Muhammad for the traumas he would face during his most tender years.

His father died shortly before his birth, and Muhammad lived with his wet nurse until he was two years old. At the tender age of six, his mother died also. He then went to live with his grandfather who died when he was eight. Muhammad was then sent to live with his uncle until he became an adult. The traditions of the culture wouldn't allow his uncle to provide him with anything beyond prevention from starvation. As a result, Muhammad never learned to read or write, but he did learn the trade routes and the lay of the land by accompanying his uncle, who was a tradesman, on his business ventures where he became well-known by the people who would ensure his future.

As an adult, Muhammad utilized this training and ran his own trade caravan as far north as Syria. On one of these business ventures, he met one of his many wives, Khadijah, a wealthy Christian merchant who was fifteen years his senior. Her wealth allowed him to retreat to the cave of Hira and fast for days, or weeks, at a time as he meditated and reflected on his life and the many gods in the Kaaba. (The Kaaba still exists today, and Muslims are required to visit it once in their lifetime on a religious journey called Hajj.)

During these retreats, Muhammad received visions and visitations, which later became the Quran. This book is comparable to the Bible, and Muslims must abide by its requirements. His Christian wife, Khadijah, took Muhammad to her Christian cousin, Nofi, after Muhammad had received his first visitation, to seek counsel about it. Nofi convinced Muhammad that

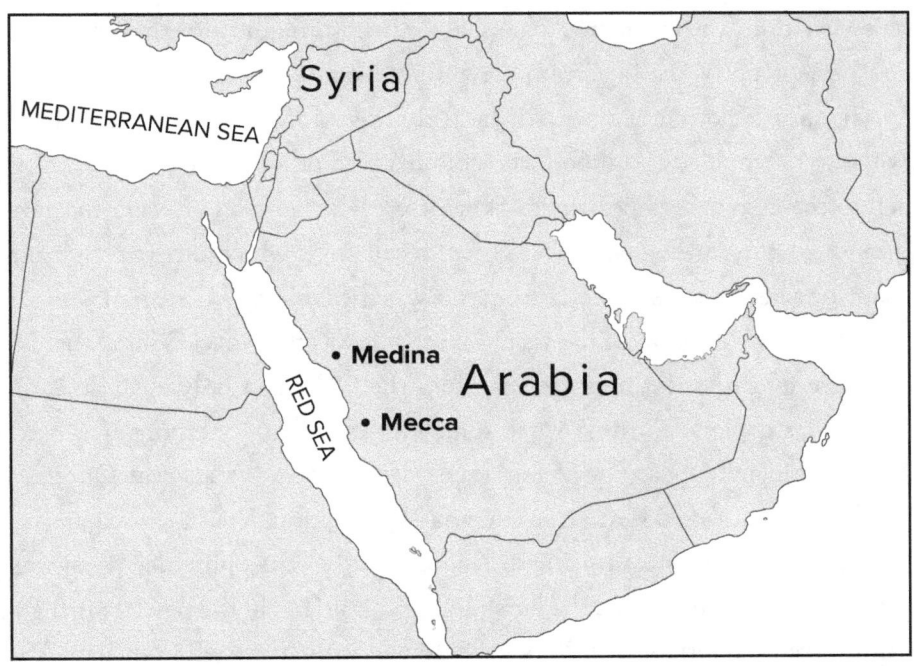

Kaaba where Muslims are required to visit once in their lifetime.

this visitation was from the Angel Gabriel who brought him the latest and most uncorrupted message from the God of his forefather, Abraham.

It's worth noting here, that if he truly existed, Muhammad was a man with a very troubled childhood who couldn't read or write and subjected himself to the extreme temperatures of the desert with no food or water for days and weeks at a time when he was visited by an angel who didn't proclaim his name or whom his message was from. He was then told by a Christian woman, who wasn't present during the visitation, that it was the Angel Gabriel that he had seen and that this message was from the ONE and only TRUE GOD. These facts demand the answers to some very important questions that need to be considered by every reader, not only of this book, but also the Quran.

Had he subjected himself to such harsh conditions that it caused a physical reaction in his body causing delusions? Was he schizophrenic? What was Nofi's childhood like? Had the harsh living conditions in the desert, during a famine, caused both of their lives to be dramatically impacted in their youth? Did they both have an unfulfilled need for validation or was God validating them? Had he truly connected with God himself or another spirit being that wasn't from God?

After all, at the onset, it wasn't the words in the Quran that validated it as being the latest and most uncorrupted message from God, or that Muhammad was his prophet, but the words of a Christian woman who not only wasn't present during the visitations but also did not hold any office or position of authority. Does this sound familiar to how Eve deceived Adam? Both Adam and Eve had direct relationships with God, but it was the woman who deceived Adam and convinced him that the serpent was right and that it was God who was deceiving them both.

Muhammad began spreading "the word of God" throughout Mecca and gained many converts. He proclaimed that it was no different from Christian or Jewish teachings but rather an extension of them to replace their old, corrupted, and no longer relevant doctrines. His proclamation didn't bode well with the tribal, religious, and commerce leaders in Mecca, and they saw it as a direct threat. Muhammad taught a minimalist lifestyle that threatened commerce and a one god ideology that threatened traffic to Mecca from travelers who came to worship their gods housed in the Kaaba. Rumors got back to Muhammad of a plot to kill him, so he fled with his followers to Medina, where rumors of his ability to "hear from God" had also spread.

He was welcomed to Medina as an authority who would settle all disputes, a judge of sorts. Now Muhammad was not only a prophet, but a judge as well, with no system of checks and balances. Soon though, he would take on another role, in addition to those. He received new visions that contradicted his original teachings. These new visions said it was okay to attack and kill to survive or to spread Islam, so he led his followers on several raids of the trade caravans from Mecca that traveled close to Medina. Muhammad was now a military leader, a prophet, and a judge with no system of checks and balances who would soon become a political leader/dictator of sorts. He gained a lot of support too by teaching that women can have jobs and should be welcomed and respected in every commerce position and at home.

The leaders of Mecca planned an attack in retaliation for Muhammad raiding their trade caravans, and several battles ensued over the coming years. Mecca had much larger armies than Muhammad, but they had little success in defeating his smaller armies. Unable to defeat him, the leaders of Mecca decided that his visions must be from God. Mecca submitted to Muhammad, so he led an army of his followers to Mecca and destroyed all the gods housed in the Kaaba, firmly planting the cornerstone of Islam in the religious and commercial hub of Arabia. The seed of the White Horse—religion—had now found a point of entry into its host, the Kaaba.

Forcing the rest of the tribes of Arabia to submit to Islam was next on Muhammad's agenda. During these holy wars, he had dreams that he could take women and their daughters for sex or as wives after brutally killing and beheading the men and boys who refused to submit.

They shall put you out of the synagogues: yea
the time cometh, that whosoever killeth you
will think that he doeth God a service.

John 16:4

The life of Muhammad shows that the brutal attacks on Israel by Hamas and the barbarism of other "extremist groups," like ISIS, aren't by extremist groups at all, but rather the original form of Islam. Shortly after Muhammad's death, the first caliphate was formed, and for the first time, the warring tribes of Arabia became a united force behind the Quran. Iran is now openly stating that its goal is to reunite the Arab nations into a caliphate, and it looks like these rogue terror groups are joining them in the role of carrying this cause.

Over the next few centuries, Islam spread throughout all of Arabia, by means of their holy wars, then northward into Rome. This caused the loss of many of Rome's territories to Muslim occupation, because they surrendered to no law but Islam and the Quran, and Roman laws were no exception. They captured Jerusalem around AD 635, and by AD 846 the Arab wars with Rome were well underway. This was the last of three waves of major woes that finally brought an already weak and scattered Rome to its knees. The death blows to Rome would come from the next Mediterranean empire that was forged by another man who will mount the White Horse of religion, and he will do it with a bow.

The curtains open
end of an age
light breaks forth
turning each page
bow in hand
heart of rage
a horseman gallops
onto the stage

Additional Sources

"Feeling Joy for the Birth of Prophet Muhammad." About Islam, October 27, 2020. https://aboutislam.net/reading-islam/about-muhammad/feeling -joy-birth-prophet/.

"Investigating Islam with Dr. Jay Smith (2 Corinthians 10:5)." YouTube, September 15, 2023. https://youtu.be/40DclW84HkM?si=8bTc2GIYAsvN R7Ml.

"Muhammad: Legacy of a Prophet." PBS. Accessed January 10, 2024. https:// www.pbs.org/muhammad/timeline_html.shtml.

Timmons, Greg. "Muhammad." Biography. Accessed January 10, 2024. https://www.biography.com/religious-figures/muhammad.

Wall, William, and Nicholai Sinai. "Muhammad." Encyclopaedia Britannica, January 1, 2024. https://www.britannica.com/biography/Muhammad.

Wikipedia Contributors. "Byzantine–Arab Wars (780–1180)." Wikipedia, The Free Encyclopedia. April 21, 2024. https://en.wikipedia.org/wiki /Byzantine%E2%80%93Arab_wars_%28780%E2%80%931180%29.

Osman Gazi, Father of the Ottoman Empire, reign AD 1299 – 1324

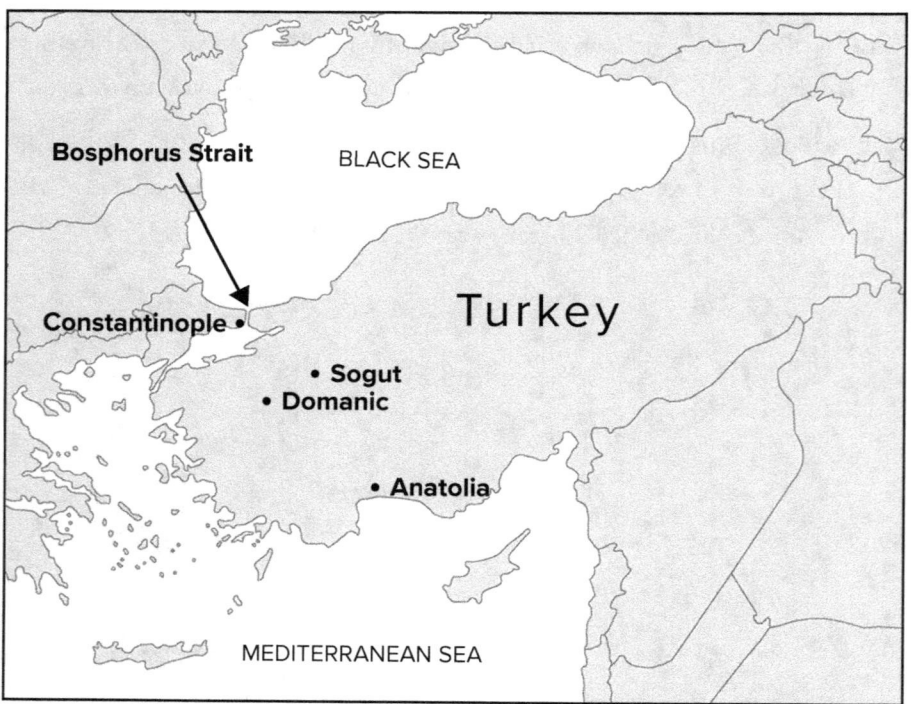

Osman Gazi's original territory included only the cities of Sogut and Domanic.

Chapter 4

Horsing: A Round with Rome

And I (John) saw (when the first seal was opened) and behold
(1) a white horse:
(2) and he that sat on him had a bow:
and (3) a crown was given unto him:
and (4) he went forth conquering and to conquer.
Revelation 6:2

His name was Osman Gazi, born in AD 1258 to Ertugral Gazi, and he was next in line to be the king of the Kayi tribe of Sunni Muslims. In AD 1281, his father died, and at twenty-three years of age, Osman became the new king of the Kayi tribe. "…A crown was given unto him." Osman is known as the father of the Ottoman Empire, the empire soon to encompass the eastern Mediterranean seaboard and replace Rome as the next world power.

Osman's tribe had lived a nomadic existence, with their flocks and herds between Sogut and Domanic, on the plateaus of Anatolia (Turkey), just south of Rome's capitol. Gazi means "a warrior of the Islamic faith." "…Behold, a white horse." Their tribe was known for being highly skilled horsemen, who were experts at wielding a sword, spending hours every day practicing and passing these skills along to the young men of the tribe. More importantly, they were known for their ability to skillfully use the short bow while riding horses to initiate sudden and quick attacks on their enemies. This skill required immense arm and upper body strength just to pull the bow back, let alone on horseback while aiming the bow. "…He that sat on him had a bow." This skill gave them a distinct military advantage as they rushed on horseback into unsuspecting villages of tribes and shot their bows from the safety of a moving horse. (The short bow is much more powerful than a regular bow and is extremely hard to draw back.)

Looming storm clouds had been gathering around the tribe of the new king for some time, much like we are watching gather around us as I write this book in 2023. No matter what country you are in, you can feel the effects of wars taking place or getting ready to take place or you are watching more holy wars. Many entities are once again striving around the great Mediterranean, and one of them will soon rise to be the next world power.

Around AD 635, when the holy wars of Islam captured Jerusalem, the geographic center of the world, the young lions marked their territory by planting the shrine of Islam in the Holy City around AD 685, known today as the Dome of the Rock. As the spread of Islam continued to weaken and threaten Rome, the (Catholic) Church of Rome took decisive action against this new threat to their country and their religion.

In AD 1096, the Church of Rome launched their own holy wars that we know as "The Crusades." Two holy wars were now in progress. The Christians sought to retake the Holy City of Jerusalem from the Muslims while the Muslims just sought any new territory to add to their caliphate. In addition to Rome's threat from the west, the new king in AD 1281 was facing the Mongols advancing from the East. The Mongols were the greatest and largest land-based empire of that day, and their sites were now set on conquering the lands around Great Mediterranean Sea as well.

These approaching storm clouds had to be confronted, so Osman gathered the strongest, most skilled, and reckless men of his tribe before heading

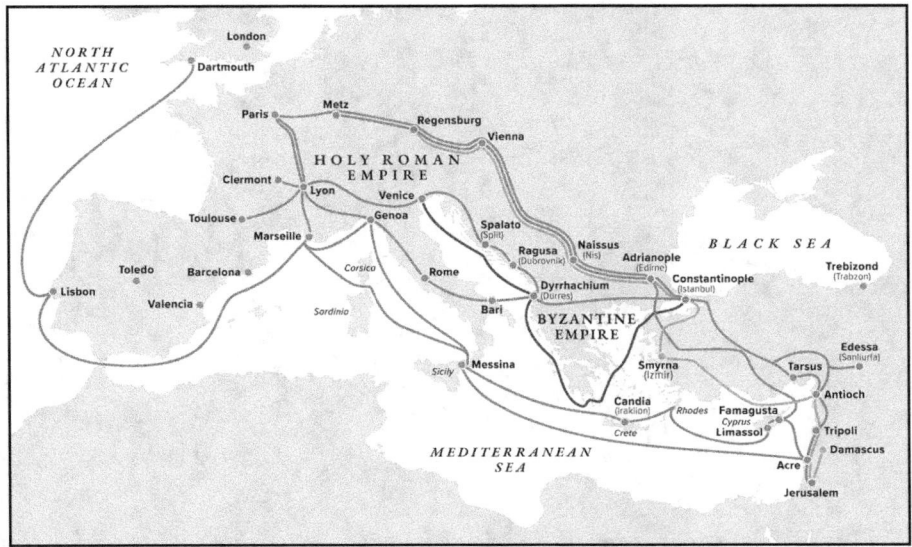

The Crusades advanced toward the West while the Mongols invaded the area around the Black Sea.

out to carve a larger territory for him to rule and to supply more men in his army. Osman's men quickly became known as the "Terror of the World." They rushed in, undetected, on horseback shooting flaming arrows into the homes or at anyone in the streets, and the speed of their attacks couldn't be matched.

> Before them a fire devoureth;
> And behind them a flame burneth…
>
> Joel 2:3

Osman then led his small army of four hundred Islamic warriors to war with approaching Mongol armies. "…He went forth conquering…" After turning the Mongol armies back, he set his face to conquer the Byzantines and squelch The Crusades "…and to conquer." By AD 1307, he had four thousand Islamic warriors, and by around AD 1323, when he died, he had conquered the large territory that surrounded the southern border of Constantinople. His son Orhan became the new king and the first Sultan of the

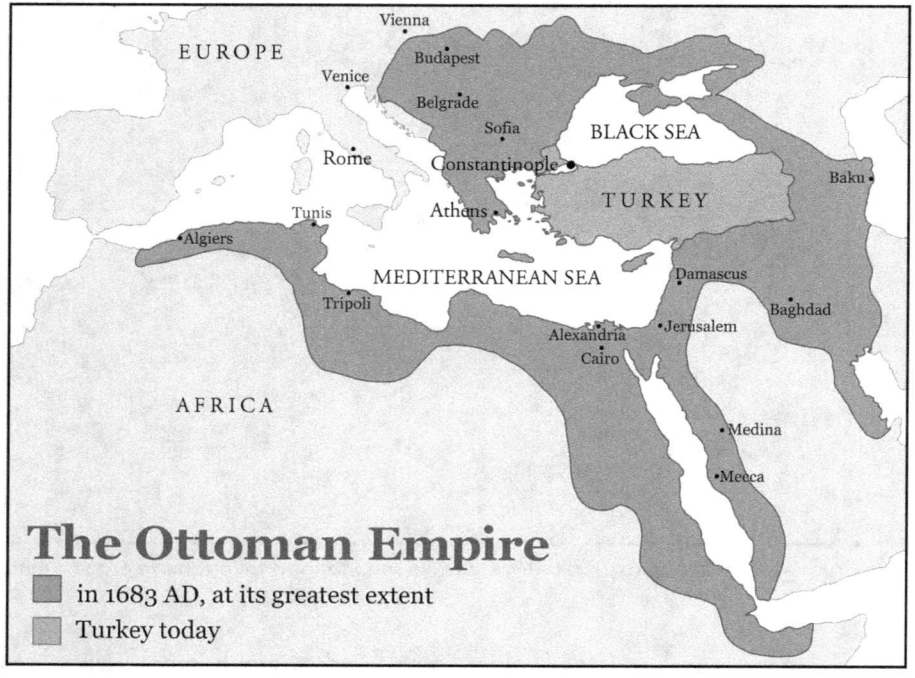

The Ottoman Empire

■ in 1683 AD, at its greatest extent
■ Turkey today

Ottoman Empire. This title would be handed down from generation to generation of heirs to the throne.

Orhan spent sixteen years expanding the territory westward, conquering the capital of his new empire, Bursa. As he conquered, he took all boys above the age of twelve that were fit, converted them to Islam, tattooed them with a number and a symbol, and then sent them for intense education and training in his army. When Orhan died around 1389, his youngest son became king. It was May 29, 1453, when the tenth Sultan, Mehmet II, finally conquered Constantinople, the last bastion of the Byzantine Empire. The golden age and era of most expansion began for the Ottoman Empire, and the Roman Empire was officially dead.

An era of growth and transformation for the Ottoman Empire began and lasted until around AD 1700. Culture began to form with amazingly beautiful architecture and trade with Europeans, who loved their spices and textiles. The sultans had conquered about half of the area around the Mediterranean from Europe to North Africa and much of the Middle East. Unfortunately, during this time period is when the Industrial Revolution began in Europe, leaving the Ottoman Empire behind and causing a long era of stagnation followed by a decline that continued until the empire's dissolution that took place from AD 1908–1922. The Ottoman Empire wasn't conquered though; it was surrendered and then divided into the Middle East nations we see today. But what caused them to surrender their great empire? The answer is that they joined forces with "The rider of the Red Horse." Two horsemen are about to be on the stage at the same time.

The Germanics played a significant role in the fall of the Roman Empire and also played a central role in the fall of the Ottoman Empire. Germany will try to rise as the next world power and will cause such carnage that the Black Horse will rise to stomp out the Red Horsemen and, in the process, will inadvertently take out the White Horse and his rider as well.

Another horseman's

evil deals

opening the

next of seals

in the effort

to give birth

he took peace

from the earth

Additional Sources

Archerybull. "Shortbow vs Longbow." Archery Bull, November 10, 2022. https://archerybull.com/shortbow-vs-longbow/.

Clark, Edward C. "The Ottoman Industrial Revolution." Cambridge Core, January 29, 2009. https://www.cambridge.org/core/journals/international-journal-of-middle-east-studies/article/abs/ottoman-industrial-revolution/A3F9C188B74F4DD9626E9879BD7122D4.

"History of the Turkish and Ottoman Empire History Channel Documentary." YouTube, February 6, 2016. https://youtu.be/ruxtynukEzw?si=LecxFzsLTWUHfIXl.

Khan, Syed Muhammad. "Battles & Conquests of the Ottoman Empire (1299-1683)." World History Encyclopedia, June 29, 2021. https://www.worldhistory.org/article/1791/battles--conquests-of-the-ottoman-empire-1299-1683/.

"Military Organization." Encyclopædia Britannica. Accessed January 23, 2024. https://www.britannica.com/place/Ottoman-Empire/Military-organization.

Notes

_____

_____

_____

_____

_____

_____

_____

_____

_____

_____

_____

_____

_____

_____

Kaiser Wilhelm II, Emperor of Germany from 1888–1918

Chapter 5

Blood Reign

And when he had opened the second seal…there went out another
(1) horse that was red: and
(2) power was given him that sat thereon to take peace from
the earth, and that they should kill one another: and
(3) there was given unto him a great sword.
Revelation 6:4

Time magazine called it "the war that ended peace"—"power was given him to take peace from the earth." Germany called the unhinged man who created the instability of World War 1 the bombastic Kaiser Wilhelm II, Emperor of Germany (Prussia). Born to Prince Fredrick William of Prussia and Princess Royal Victoria of the United Kingdom on January 27, 1859, he was the eldest grandchild of Queen Victoria of the UK and successor to Germany's throne.

Like Muhammad, Wilhelm faced an extremely troubled childhood from birth to adulthood. His entire life seems to have foreshadowed him as the rider of the Red Horse. He was a crippled heir to the throne among a regime that prized physical perfection and a royal family that demanded it. Many Germans were steeped in the identity of the Germanic Warrior who had helped defeat Rome and Wilhelm was no exception. His unfulfilled needs for validation and the lessons he learned from his childhood suffering played out in WWI with over twenty million deaths and even more injuries. After the war, he was exiled to the Netherlands and rejected by society every step of the way until he died four years after his exile. "...And there went out another horse that was red." (This writer can't do justice to Wilhelm's story, so my recommendation is that you stop at some point and watch the video source link titled "The Great War" series.)

A breech delivery had forced the doctors' use of forceps, wrenching the left arm of the future emperor and making it useless. His parents tried every treatment science had to offer from a neck brace to electric shock. With no success, they turned to a harsh tutor, hoping he could succeed where science had failed. As an adult, Wilhelm recounted the memories of his treatments as useless suffering and torture. Tutor Georg Ernst Hinzpeter showed no mercy for young Wilhelm's disability and started training the young prince at eight years old to execute the most important skill for an emperor to have during that era—riding a horse. Regardless of tears or injuries, every time young Wilhelm fell off the horse, Hinzpeter picked him up, put him back on, and went through the paces again. This went on daily for weeks until the young prince could stay on the horse.

On visits to his grandmother, Queen Victoria, in Great Britain, Wilhelm played war games with his cousins. She had a battlefield built for the royal children with forts and trenches where they could play just off the coast of her island estate. The royal family, including his uncle the Prince of Wales, found the young prince to be an insufferable bully because he always had to win, at any cost, and this would play out in his adult life as well. He became obsessed with war, war ships, and the sea. On his visits to England, he visited their great fleet of navy ships in Portsmouth and Plymouth vowing to have such a great navy fleet as theirs when he was in power. As he grew to adulthood, his complexes became too complex for the royal family to deal with, but soon, society would have to deal with them as well, and then the rest of the world.

At the age of eighteen, Wilhelm joined the army. He felt he had finally found his home and the respect he didn't get growing up, oblivious to the fact that no officer dare dispute with or criticize the heir to the throne. His ego continued to be fed by his comrades until his father died in AD 1888. At the age of twenty-nine, he became the Emperor of Germany, with a fully cemented superego and a realization that his childhood obsessions were no longer on the distant horizon but firmly in the grasp of his only good hand. In the other hand, he hid his disability by always holding a sword.

The foreshadowing of how things were going to play out is uncanny. He had been taught to hold the reins and stay in the saddle through any unforeseen turbulence, so he did, but he never realized he was the one creating his own turbulence. Ironically, Sigmund Freud was working on publishing his psychoanalysis of the superego that develops in the first five years of life based on parental moral standards.

Wilhelm's first order of business was to remove the stirrups from the figurative horse he had mounted. He sent the only voice of reason who had maintained balance and peace in the region, Germany's Chancellor Otto von Bismarck, into retirement. Bismarck had masterfully forged Germany into a country in 1871 by unifying its people, and he maintained peace in the region by offering friendship to three of the five major countries that surrounded it. The five included Russia, Britain, France, Austria-Hungary, and Italy, and he had a well-established friendship with Russia, Britain, and France.

After sending Bismarck into retirement, Wilhelm began alienating all his allies. He forced Britain into a defensive posture by publicly boasting that he would create a naval force greater than theirs. His words sparked an arms race among not only the European nations but the rest of the world as well. He built the greatest army in Europe, causing Russia to take a defensive posture and to forge an alliance with France. Now, the emperor's only friend was the small, unstable nation of Austria-Hungary.

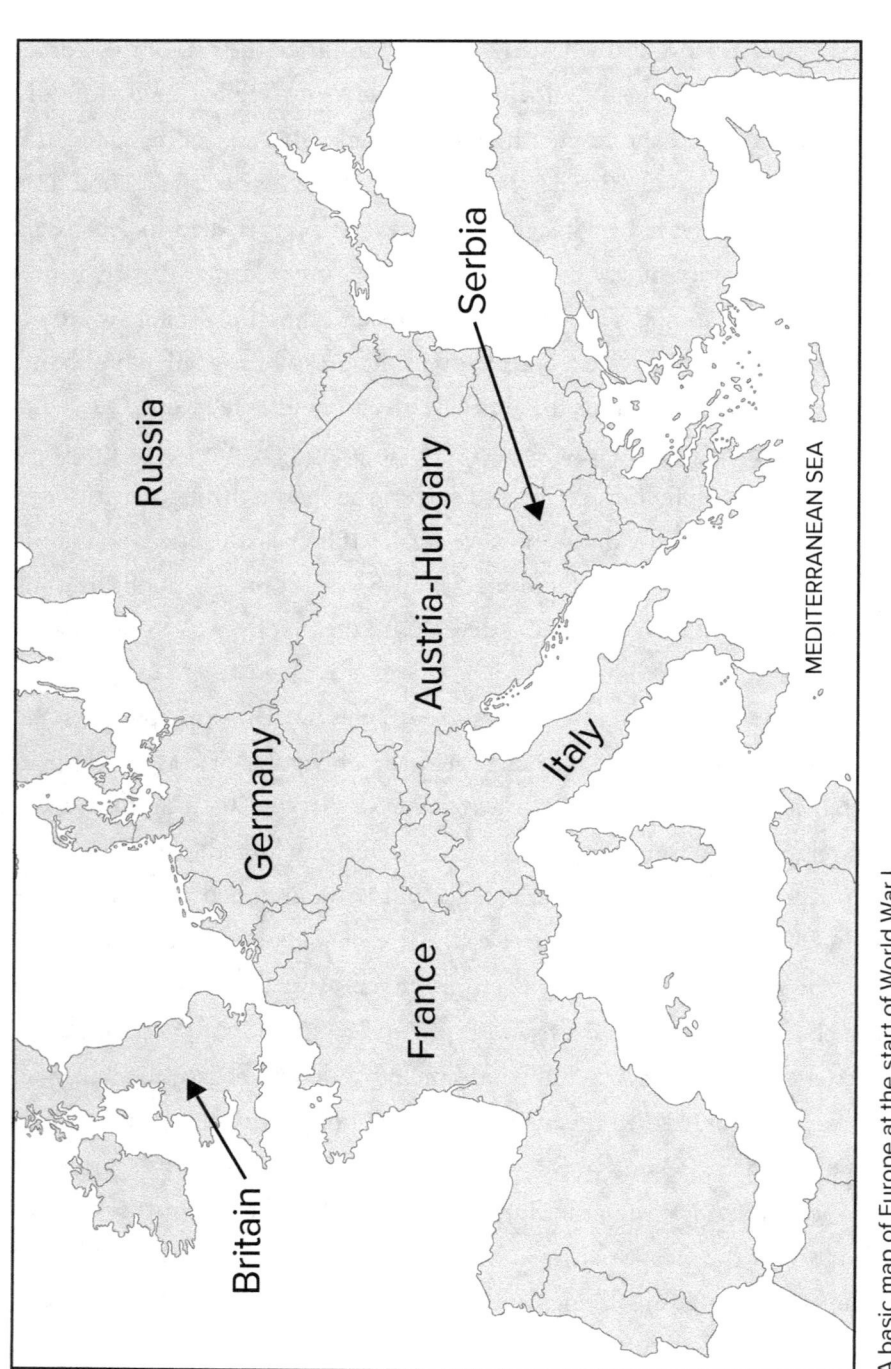

A basic map of Europe at the start of World War I.

The world watched as Wilhelm built a massive military during an era of explosion in technology and the Industrial Revolution. They all knew that none of them could match it. "…And a great sword was given him." A massive need for oil was created by this new era with its gas-powered engines, and the Black Horseman was quietly working off the radar to supply this need. The need for oil would soon explode when Wilhelm made yet another fatal mistake—launching WW1. He would face the war alone, with no one to back him up, as the only unstable friend he had left beckoned to him for help.

Austria-Hungary was a nation with numerous ethnic groups that had kept it unstable for some time, and one of these groups were the Slavs, whose base was centered in Serbia. It's a lot like Israel's instability today in having so many ethnic groups, one of which are the Palestinians. The Slavs wanted their independence just as much as the Palestinians want the land of Israel. The Palestinians elected what might be considered a terrorist organization, called Hamas, to do their dirty deeds, and the Slavs formed their own terrorist organization, known as "The Black Hand." Just like The Black Hand was based in Serbia, the base of Hamas is believed to be centered in, and supported by, Iran. It seems that history is repeating itself.

On June 28, 1914, heir to the Austrian throne, Archduke Franz Ferdinand and his wife, Sophia, went to visit the capital of Bosnia-Herzegovina, formerly annexed by Austria-Hungary. The Black Hand took responsibility for their assassination during this visit, and Austria-Hungary wanted vengeance. Austria's Emperor Franz Joseph went to Wilhelm for help, leading to an alliance from which Wilhelm could not retreat. Wilhelm pledged his support to Emperor Joseph to eliminate the political element of Serbia that threatened him. All of Europe would soon be obligated to take up arms because of the alliances that had been forged through Wilhelm's massive ego during his early days on the throne.

Eager to rid itself of the Slav problem with the backing of the greatest military in the world, Austria-Hungary declared war on Serbia on July 31,

1914. Wilhelm was forced to put his military where his mouth was with no major allies. Russia was then forced to take up arms against Austria-Hungary and Germany. Russia's war with Germany meant that Germany would also face France and Great Britain. Wilhelm was now riding his horse at a gallop with no stirrups and dragging all of Europe behind him by their necks on a rope of alliances. He did manage to pick up one other alliance three months into the war though—the White Horseman of the Ottoman Empire. On October 31, 1914, the Ottoman Empire joined WWI, siding with Germany, but this will prove to be a fatal mistake.

While these two horsemen were galloping side by side, suddenly there was a stalemate with both sides dug into trenches, unable to advance for nearly three years. The only good news, up to this point, was that the British had captured Jerusalem from the Muslims. During the war, Wilhelm had publicly flaunted his lavish lifestyle of house parties, hunting, and eating extravagantly while his country suffered with great destitution and loss.

Two of Wilhelm's generals decided to strip him of his power but leave him as a public figurehead. Paul Von Hindenburg and Mastermind Erich Ludendorff, two of Wilhelm's generals, forcefully seized control of Germany's military. After the war, they would force a dictatorship on Germany with Ludendorff at the helm, paving the way for Hitler, the next rider of the Red Horse, and WWII. But in this war, they made a grave error that unleashed the Black Horseman, who would not only end the stalemate and the war but stop both the Red and the White Horsemen in their tracks.

The generals decided the only way to defeat Britain was to starve them and in turn to starve their armies, so they sent their great naval fleet to sink all ships seeking entry to all of Germany's opposing allies. One of these ships was the infamous Lusitania. In addition to sinking numerous US ships full of weapons and supplies for the belligerents, the two generals reached out to Mexico, asking them to join the mayhem and declare war on America in return for Texas, New Mexico, and Arizona. This communication was called the Zimmermann Telegram, but the US intercepted it.

The US alleged that it had secured rights to ship to the belligerents without the threat of war or attack and were thriving with record profits from raw goods, weapons, and loans. Now, not only were their ships full of goods being sunk by Germany, but their borders were being threatened along with their democracy. The United States had to act and do it quickly. Americans began persecuting its German citizens, and this threat launched a race war that included blacks. Much like when Hamas attacked Israel on October 7, 2023, Jews, their homes, and businesses along Jewish organizations were targeted and sometimes killed or injured worldwide when Israel began its devastating offensive in the Gaza Strip.

An injured boy

never a man

learned to ride

but never to stand

bringing the world

to its knees

three horsemen ride

but No One Seas

Additional Sources

Collinson, Stephen. "Analysis: A New Wave of Antisemitism Threatens to Rock an Already Unstable World | CNN Politics." CNN, October 31, 2023. https://www.cnn.com/2023/10/31/politics/antisemitism -unstable-world-analysis/index.html.

"Family Tree of Emperor Wilhelm II of Prussia." Geneanet. Accessed January 23, 2024. https://gw.geneanet.org/comrade28?lang=en&n =prussia&oc=0&p=emperor%2Bwilhelm%2Bii%2Bof.

"The Great War Episode 1 Explosion." YouTube, June 26, 2012. https://youtu. be/DRtdSoeYQYk?si=s_GyalRIGUoJE1Oa.

Mougel, Nadège. "World War I Casualties." United States Census Bureau. https://www.census.gov/history/pdf/reperes112018.pdf.

"Ottoman Empire Enters the First World War." NZ History. Accessed January 23, 2024. https://nzhistory.govt.nz/war/ottoman-empire/enters-the -war.

"Superego." Encyclopaedia Britannica. https://www.britannica.com/science /superego.

"The Zimmermann Telegram." National Archives and Records Administration. Article adapted from: Alexander, Mary and Marilyn Childress. "The Zimmerman Telegram." Social Education 45, 4 (April 1981): 266 https://www.archives.gov/education/lessons/zimmermann.

Chapter 6

Horsing: A Round with Germany

Revelation 6:5–6 — ...And when he had opened the third seal...I beheld,
and lo 1) A black horse; and he that sat on him had
2) a pair of balances (scales) in his hand
And I heard a voice in the midst of the four beasts say,
1) A measure of wheat for a penny,
2) and three measures of barley for a penny;
3) and see thou hurt not the oil
4) and the wine.

Woodrow Wilson was very familiar with the carnage of war. As a child, he witnessed America's Civil War and watched his mother tend to wounded soldiers. He saw WWI as Europe's civil war and ran his 1917 second bid for the US presidency on the platform of "isolationism from Europe's war." WWI took over twenty million lives and left more than twenty-one million casualties. More importantly, it shifted the centralized power bases from the East to the West. The empires of the Great Mediterranean Sea will no longer dominate the world because a new world power is emerging that is based on capitalism and oil that is backed by military might.

The wealthy tycoons who employed America's workers and financed

Woodrow Wilson's second campaign for the presidency were experiencing huge losses from the war. Their major investments in Europe were in danger of collapsing if Germany won the war, and it appeared that Germany would win if America didn't intervene. Europe had gone through all their able men and were now drafting boys and older men. America knew that Mexico was no threat to America's military, but Woodrow Wilson succumbed to the pressure from the tycoons and decided to use the Zimmermann Telegram, along with the repeated sinking of its U-boats by Germany, as an excuse to enter the war. He had to protect not only the investments of the men who had paid for his campaign, but the booming American economy as well.

Much like Muhammad preceded and paved the way for the White Horseman, Woodrow Wilson preceded and paved the way for the Black Horseman to launch America as the next greatest world power. America's oil industry carried him just as the religion of Islam carried the White Horseman. Had it not been for the oil rush of 1859 in Texas, none of it would have taken place. "…And I beheld, and lo, a black horse (oil)."

America was in an era of prosperity and growth from the Industrial Revolution, the gold rush of 1848, and the oil rush of 1859. The future was not only uncertain for the East but was also threatening the economy and stability of the West. On April 2, 1917, Woodrow Wilson appeared before Congress asking for a declaration of war against Germany and the Axis powers in the east. Two days later, America entered the war, turning Europe's civil war into a world war. News of the Zimmermann Telegram and the sinking of U-boats sparked race wars against Germans living in America. Americans began attacking Germans on every level possible. (The same thing happened worldwide against Jews with the Israel-Hamas War of 2023. Worldwide antisemitism soared to an all-time high as Jews experienced harassment in US colleges, their homes sprayed with swastikas in Germany, and even physical attacks, just to list a few.)

The United States was still perfecting its legal system to uphold the pledge of its flag "With Liberty and Justice for All." It was George Washington who had signed the Judiciary Act of 1789 into law, establishing the Federal Court System, symbolized by "the scales of justice." "…And he that sat on him had a pair of balances in his hand." There are several speculations about the interpretations of the "pair of balances" held by the rider and the color of the Black Horse, but no matter what interpretation you hold, America fulfilled them all (and maybe all or more than one of them apply). They will all be addressed in the next few chapters, and you will see "…And he that sat on him had a pair of balances in his hand" repeated, with explanation, throughout the chapters. However, the most literal and simplest interpretation for the balances in the hand of the rider is the scales of justice.

Great Britain expected America to feed its troops into the failing British war machine under Great Britain's control, but America refused and controlled their own troops. Most history books overlook the fact that it was America's intervention that ended WWI, but a writer at Time Magazine felt that credit went to America for saving the day. France was down to three million men and mutiny was in the air with half of them refusing to attack German armies leaving the other half demoralized. Britain was down to two million men who were facing a constant influx of fresh German soldiers, with crushing military superiority, coming to the front in droves from the battles that had recently defeated Russia and Italy. At best, both France and Britain were staggering into the end of 1917.

By the winter of 1917, America drafted a million men and sent them to France. Germany had advanced their armies just fifty miles from the border of Paris. By April 1918, Germany had British armies with nowhere to look but up. During the spring and summer of 1918, America's additional million volunteers and two million more draftees caused both German fronts to fall, but it was America's Doughboys that dealt the final blow to Germany.

The battle of Meuse-Argonne lasted from September 26, 1918, to November 11, 1918. The US Doughboys had managed to trap German armies in France and Belgium, cutting off their supply line. On November 11, 1918, WWI was over, the United States was now recognized as the greatest military world power, and Kaiser Wilhelm, along with a few other high-ranking individuals, skulked quietly out of the country in shame and fear. The child, who had been injured by a doctor and tortured by his parents, with no balance, and whose cries were ignored by his tutor, who insisted he learn the skill of staying on his horse with no stirrups, had fallen off his horse. A new horseman was galloping onto the world stage, and now we must travel back in time again to hear what Daniel says about God's interpretation of "balances."

In Daniel 5, we learn the origin of a phrase commonly used today to describe the indicators of an unavoidable event on the horizon: "The Handwriting on the Wall." Belshazzar, king of Babylon, was having a big party. In his drunken state, he commanded that the gold and silver vessels his father had taken from the temple of the Jews, when he seized Jerusalem, be brought out so that everyone at his party could drink from them. As the party raged on, with the gold and silver vessels in the hands of his guests, Belshazzar praised the gods of Babylon. Within the hour, a hand appeared in everyone's view and brought the party to a screeching halt as it wrote these words on a nearby wall: "Thou art weighed in the balances and found wanting (lacking). God hath numbered thy kingdom and finished it; Thy kingdom is divided and given to the Medes and the Persians." Within twenty-four hours, the Medes and the Persians attacked Babylon, and the kingdom of Babylon came to its end.

Some scholars, preachers, and teachers believe that the balances in the hand of the Black Horseman represent judgment on a nation or empire, but to others, the balances represent judgment on two nations or empires. When America rose to power, they fulfilled both. You will see that in this chapter and the next as America takes the White Horse and his rider out of the running and leaves the Red Horse too weak to run and with no rider to boot. The Ottoman Empire would soon be divided, just as the handwriting on the wall predicted for Babylon. "...Thy kingdom is divided."

After Germany's humiliating defeat, the Ottoman Empire was seized by the British and French and divided between them in the 1916 secret Sykes-Picot Agreement and the 1919 Peace Treaty of Versailles. The Ottoman Empire was officially dead, without ever being invaded or attacked, and it was dead for joining forces with Germany in WWI. Over time, the Middle East nations we see today were born, replacing the Ottoman Empire. (Highlight those two facts because they will play a huge role in defining other forces at play in the Book of Revelation, which will be clarified in the next book in this series.)

Both treaties neglected to mention highly disputed territories and indiscriminately added borders to define these new countries. As a result, the new boundaries forced opposing people groups into territories that became ruled by a single government. These borders remain as a source of contention in the Middle East and have created many of the wars and uprisings that continue today.

As part of the treaties, Britain received Jordan, southern Iraq, and Haifa in Israel. France got Syria, Lebanon, northern Iraq, Mosul, and southeast Turkey, including Kurdistan and part of Palestine. Here is a list of how the former Ottoman Empire was divided and the birthdates of the Islamic nations in the Middle East:

- Jordan became a nation under the British protectorate in 1921 and gained independence in 1946.
- Northern Iraq became a nation under the British protectorate in 1921 and gained its independence from both France and Britain in 1932.
- Syria gained independence from France in 1946.
- Lebanon gained its independence from France in 1956.

- Turkey became a nation and gained its independence from France in 1923.
- Kurdistan is still waiting to be recognized as a nation but emerged in 1992 with its own government and parliament.
- Haifa is part of Israel, and Israel was born in 1948.
- Iran became a Muslim country conquering Imperial Persia in 1979.
- Libya became a country in 1951.
- Egypt became a country in 1922.
- Greece became a country in 1922.
- Saudi Arabia became a country in 1932.
- Turkey became a country in 1923.

Highlight this list as a reference for the next book in this series. It's worth noting here that these are all key players in the theater of drama that has been escalating during our lifetime.

Here is quick summary of the horse race for global domination from the time of Rome and John's prophecy in the book of Revelation through the 1920s:

- The White Horse and his rider, or global conquest on the back of religion, conquered and replaced Rome as the new world power and is no longer in the race.
- The Red Horse and his rider, or global conquest on the back of war, joined by the White Horseman, is left crippled by The Black Horse and his rider.
- The Black Horseman, on the back of the oil industry, is about to launch his conquest as the next global power while it revels in the glorious Roaring 20s.
- The Red Horse is trying to regather and reform itself to relaunch, as its rider has gone into exile in the Netherlands.

The race is on
Black takes the lead
White is down
Red left in need
life goes on
in the lees
with the roaring 20s
still, No One Seas

Additional Sources

Chen, James. "Petrodollars: Definition, History, Uses." Investopedia, July 19, 2022. https://www.investopedia.com/terms/p/petrodollars.asp.

"Federal Judiciary Act (1789)." National Archives and Records Administration, n.d. https://www.archives.gov/milestone-documents/federal-judiciary-act#:~:text=One%20of%20the%20first%20acts,of%20their%20most%20important%20tasks.

"Global Connections: The Middle East - Timeline." PBS, n.d. https://www.pbs.org/wgbh/globalconnections/mideast/timeline/text/time3.html.

Latson, Jennifer. "History of the American Oil Industry: When Drake Struck Oil." Time, August 27, 2015. https://time.com/4008544/american-oil-well-history/.

"The Meuse-Argonne Offensive." National Archives and Records Administration, n.d. https://www.archives.gov/research/military/ww1/meuse-argonne.

"Most Corrupt II: Woodrow Wilson - Forgotten History." YouTube, August 28, 2023. https://youtu.be/IWwkx0a7Fdk?si=WIeUkSCpdrgga3iA.

"Sykes-Picot Agreement." Encyclopaedia Britannica, July 20, 1998. https://www.britannica.com/event/Sykes-Picot-Agreement.

Tikkanen, Amy. "California Gold Rush." Encyclopaedia Britannica, October 20, 2016. https://www.britannica.com/topic/California-Gold-Rush.

Wawro, Geoffrey. "How America Saved the Day in World War One." Time, September 26, 2018. https://time.com/5406235/everything-you-know-about-how-world-war-i-ended-is-wrong/.

Chapter 7

The Daze of Change

As a member of the army under Wilhelm during WWI, Adolf Hitler carried messages to the front lines, receiving metals for being partially blinded by mustard gas and taking shrapnel to his leg. But his childhood had left him with much deeper wounds, for which he had received no medals of honor, causing an extreme need for validation, much like Wilhelm's childhood had left him. Hitler's father was a military man and staunch in his physical and emotional abuse of the young boy. This played out in his adult life with him causing over fifty million deaths in World War Two (WWII), almost three times the deaths of WWI. It was the most devastating war in recorded history.

The Red Horse of Germany needed a new rider who could deliver a new grazing field for the weakened horse. Hitler was desperate to meet his need for validation and wanted nothing more than to mount that horse, lead it to victory, and be the hero that his father never saw and the savior that Germany so desperately needed. It was a match made in hell. It seems that Germany hadn't read Sigmund Freud's memo on the superego yet or learned the lesson about putting another superego, like Wilhelm, in power.

Born in Austria-Hungary, Hitler had seven siblings, three of which died as infants and a younger brother whose death had a profound psychological effect on him. He never paid attention in school, and his poor grades reflected it. The only things that could hold Hitler's attention were books about war, and he devoured them. At the age of thirteen, when his father died, Hitler dropped out of school. Later, as a young adult, he moved out from his mother and ended up homeless, surviving as a painter. He had a vision of reuniting Austria with Germany and ridding them of all races that weren't Aryan. In 1913, at the age of twenty-four, he moved to Germany to pursue that vision, and a year later, when WWI broke out, he joined the army. He shared his vision for Germany with his comrades at every opportunity and became popular with many high- and low-ranking personnel.

After WWI, Germany was saddled with huge reparations and restricted army size and weapons, along with a loss of territory along its borders. Numerous groups broke out, all claiming to have the answer to the problems that Germany faced, and one of them was the Nazi Party. In 1925, Hitler took a low-level government job with the Nazi Party that gave him automatic citizenship, and it was here that Hitler finally found the validation he so desperately needed to fully cement his superego. While Hitler gained popularity in the Nazi Party, Germany was in chaos as warring parties took over the streets and the country went through several forms of government, all promising solutions. America, though, was reveling in a boom that led to another era of prosperity called "The Roaring Twenties."

American businesses boomed in numbers and the New York stock market soared as a result. People began spending their paychecks on stocks and reaping the benefits on almost a daily basis. Cities grew exponentially as country dwellers sought a better life. Travel became explosive, plane and car production soared, and owning a car became the craze of Americans. Laborers were cheap with a large influx of immigrants fleeing the instability of the East in pursuit of the American Dream, leading to record production of goods and exports. America now produced 40% of the world's goods, 85% of the world's cars, and possessed two-thirds of the world's gold and half of the world's oil. Hollywood became the number one hotbed for movie production as it offered every setting for filming and always had good weather with plenty of funds to support production. Yachts began filling the harbors. Maids and butlers could now be afforded, giving major cities even more time for the party life. The invention of appliances provided more time to travel and party as well. Baseball, radio, movies, advertising, and lavish parties permeated the atmosphere as American businesses expanded overseas. Churches were growing and being built at a record pace from the Azuza Street Revival of 1906, and the gospel began to spread to unreached nations at hyper speed. America went through three presidents during the boom, but as the face of America smiled gleefully, the underbelly looked quite different.

Farm subsidies from WWI were cut off, causing a boom of foreclosures. The boom of big business caused a boom of privately-owned businesses to close or be foreclosed on. Coal mines closed as electricity expanded leaving numerous areas with no way to earn a living. Many moved to the big cities to survive or seek a better life. Horses were replaced with horsepower, and those with horses couldn't afford cars and had no credit. Mobster and gang wars broke out in the large cities, and they grew in power during the Prohibition with the nightlife of home parties. The KKK (Ku Klux Klan) grew to four million, lynching people without a trial.

Government corruption became rampant, and radio became an easy avenue to spread propaganda to promote and hide the government's dirty deeds. Bankers became very rich and powerful with the skyrocketing demand for credit and mass foreclosures. Corporations, banks, and mobsters slowly gained more traction with politicians than the people, and the KKK took justice into their own hands while sometimes being used by politicians, bankers, and tycoons to do so.

While WWI became a distant memory to the West, resentment from the outcome of WWI caused tensions in the East to escalate as four major totalitarian powers emerged, causing the arms race to go into high gear. Japan had its sights set on Manchuria and then China. If there ever was an unholy trinity, Germany's Hitler, Italy's Mussolini, and Russia's Stalin were it. In 1911, Italy had invaded Libya in pursuit of becoming the next Mediterranean superpower, and Mussolini had his sites set on Ethiopia and resurrecting the Roman Empire. Stalin, of Russia, had his sights set on East Europe as a route for global domination, and Germany was starting to embrace Hitler in their dire need for food and jobs. Hitler was doing what he did best—aggressive public speaking about a future of greatness for Germany (that would never materialize). While Hitler propelled himself forward in unholy alliances with Stalin and Mussolini, Japan, the lone mustang, went on its own rampage.

As he gained popularity, Hitler began his propaganda campaign by gaslighting the crowds (distorting their perception of reality). His platform was that Germany didn't lose the war. According to Hitler, it was the unfair Versailles Treaty that had saddled Germany with the starvation and lack that his listeners were enduring. He slated the unpatriotic Jews and other foreigners as the reason Germany lost the war. Hitler successfully turned the anger of the starving masses away from its leaders and toward the victors of WWI, foreigners, unsavory citizens like gays, and the Jews.

The latest form of Germany's ever-morphing government had found a way to payback war reparations by securing loans from the United States. These loans paid Germany's reparations to Europe, Britain, and others. In turn, those countries could pay the United States back for the loans they had been given to finance their countries during WWI. After almost a decade of prosperity for America and regrouping for Germany, a dark cloud suddenly covered the entire world economy without warning. No one saw it coming or, at the time, knew what had caused it.

On October 29, 1929, the New York stock market crashed, and the entire world economy came to a screeching halt launching the "Great Depression." The destitution of Germany during the last decade, suddenly seemed like a cake walk compared to what they were now facing, and this was Hitler's chance to rise to power. Many Bible scholars believe that the Black Horse, the scales in the rider's hand, and "a measure of wheat for a penny and three measures of barley for a penny" represent food scarcity and hyperinflation. A severe drought in the Midwest and southern Great Plains also caused "The Great Dust Bowl" that lasted from 1931–1940. Many lives were lost, and food scarcity hit severe levels worldwide. By 1933, both America and Germany were in dire straits when two men rose to power who would change the course of the world. In 1933, both Germany and America were mounted by new riders that would usher in the next era: "The Ride of the Black Horseman."

On March 4, 1933, Franklin D. Roosevelt was elected as the president of the United States, and on September 1, 1933, Hitler became Chancellor of the Reich in Germany. Hyperinflation, starvation, unemployment, and homelessness were rampant, and both leaders faced daunting challenges. Germany defaulted on reparation payments to Europe and Great Britain. In turn, Europe and Great Britain defaulted on their loans to America from WWI. Banks went under, businesses closed, and everything spiraled out of anyone's control. Maybe that's why no one noticed when the Pale Horse emerged in the Middle East or saw it as a threat. Even if they had noticed, no one was in any condition to stop it.

When the Ottoman Empire was divided after WWI, it came under British control and left the Muslim population resentful and feeling powerless with no leader, just as WWI had left Germany. In addition to that, the boundaries Great Britain had defined for the Middle East trapped opposing forces under one government. It created an upheaval filled with violence and a vacuum fueled by dictators and terrorist groups who wanted nothing more than to find their footing and regain their empires.

In 1928, the year before the stock market crashed, the Muslim Brotherhood was born in Egypt that now has branches bearing the fruit of terror, like Hamas along with many others. These groups are the hell that would soon arise to follow the Pale Horse. Oil became the means of power and survival in this era. This is the period in which the Black Horse grew to power, the Pale Horse was born, and once again, the rider of the Red Horse was knocked off.

From the time that Hitler came to power until his defeat and alleged suicide, it was like watching a mad Pitbull chew off two of his own legs, defy the world, go to war on the two legs he had left, attack his own tail, and then jump off a cliff. First, Hitler eliminated all his opposing forces and had them sent to concentration camps. Second, he destroyed what was left of his own economy by dealing with the "Jewish problem." (Many wealthy business owners in Germany were Jewish at that time.) Over six million Jews, socially unsavory people, and Christians were exterminated by Hitler in his quest to conquer the world and replace it with the superior Aryan race of Germans. Only God knows how many of his opponents he killed in the concentration camps. Third, during the end of his lunacy, he became paranoid and began killing his own officers, along with citizens who he feared might support them, squelching any oppositions rumored to be plotting against him. Finally, after the war, he allegedly committed suicide.

Roosevelt, however, was taking a more positive, reasonable approach and was no stranger to overcoming suffering and obstacles. This is the story, in two nutshells, of the rise of the Black Horseman and his ride upon the oil empire of the United States of America as it rose to be the next world power.

For every time
has a purpose
for every season
has its circus
a time of worst
a time of best
the sun now rises
on the West

Additional Sources

"1929 Stock Market Crash and the Great Depression - Documentary." YouTube, July 6, 2018. https://youtu.be/qlSxPouPCIM?si=zBSNuL5wmh9gF59s.

"Birth of a Führer: The Rise and Fall of Adolf Hitler: The Life of Adolf Hitler: Timeline." YouTube, March 18, 2023. https://youtu.be/pLFjw0zKcgQ?si=xh_AUEBstDpDSicy.

"Blood Money - Inside the Nazi Economy: Part 1: A World War on Credit: Free Documentary History." YouTube, December 14, 2022. https://youtu.be/IOzw3i5Nt5g?si=nPp-JoAp-Ng9XlzI.

"The Century: America's Time - The Beginning: Seeds of Change." YouTube, December 29, 2013. https://youtu.be/dssfiPirT2U?si=1Z-ODx1xhmcLDVRI.

"The Dust Bowl: Darkness in the Great Depression." YouTube, November 27, 2020. https://youtu.be/sxG6Lwkzi7c?si=GBv5sqhg5ZxjW7mU.

"The Roaring 20's: Crash Course US History #32." YouTube, October 4, 2013. https://youtu.be/VfOR1XCMf7A?si=5a2-iVMXdYD1HLIv.

"World War II." Defense Casualty Analysis System. Accessed 2024. https://dcas.dmdc.osd.mil/dcas/app/conflictCasualties/ww2.

Franklin Roosevelt, 32nd president of the United States from 1933–1945

Chapter 8

From Blood Reigns to Capital Gains

Franklin Delano Roosevelt (FDR) was a New York Senator until Woodrow Wilson appointed him as Assistant Secretary of the US Navy in 1913. While in this office, FDR's aggressive push for expansion of the navy ensured the US victory in WWI and WWII. But, in 1921, he was diagnosed with polio, causing him to spend three years learning to walk again and most of his following days in a wheelchair. Despite this tragic setback, in 1928, he ran for governor of New York and then won the presidency in 1933. His platform—"Restoration from crisis to a better day, endure, revive, prosper, nothing to fear but fear itself, turn retreat into advance"—led him to more than one landslide victory during his three terms as president of the United States.

Roosevelt turned every tragedy into triumph, and though he had difficulty walking, he was quick on his feet to respond to everything America was facing. He successfully led America through the Great Depression, the decade-long Dust Bowl, and the WWII victory against Hitler. Along with expanding the Navy that had effectively ended WWI during his time as Assistant Secretary of the US Navy under Woodrow Wilson, Roosevelt gave the next president the weapon that would defeat Japan and end WWII. He signed the legislation, made the agreements, and fostered the deals that caused America to become the next world power without acquiring or conquering new territory. He helped create the United Nations (UN) and fostered the creation of the World Bank and International Monetary Fund. It's hard to imagine where America, or the rest of the world for that matter, might be today had FDR not been president during this crucial time in history. While wars were breaking out on every front by the four ferocious phantoms of misery in the East, Roosevelt was taking numerous actions to revive, protect, and prosper America as he refused to get involved in WWII unless America was attacked.

In 1933, the box office hit, King Kong, gave Americans an escape from the harsh reality of the Depression. But the drought of 1938 created dust storms that lasted over a decade causing around seven thousand deaths, some of which were from starvation. In Stalin's Russia, farmers had resorted to cannibalism after his political attacks on their farms. Germany's Hitler sent his military and political opponents to concentration camps, and Japan's Hirohito planned invasions to get resources like oil, as his country had to import 94% of theirs. Standard Oil was drilling for oil in Saudi Arabia, and Roosevelt took several emergency actions to revive America from the Great Depression.

FDR unhinged the dollar from gold by suspending the gold standard, created Social Security payments to the elderly, started paying hurting farmers to not farm some of their land, ended the Prohibition, and created the Tennessee Valley Authority (TVA). The TVA built numerous dams to prevent catastrophic flooding in the valley and to provide cheap electricity to remote areas that had none while providing impoverished people with good paying jobs. The Tennessee Valley project was also where the notorious atom bomb was created that would later effectively end the last front of WWII against Japan's Hirohito. Hirohito had already invaded Manchuria in 1931 and was preparing to invade northern China.

While Roosevelt unhinged the dollar from gold, Hitler created his own currency, the MEFO. As Babe Ruth ended his career in 1935, Italy's Mussolini was invading Ethiopia, and Hitler notified the world that he was rearming in defiance of the Treaty of Versailles. The following year, the Arab Revolt against the British Mandate from WWI began in Palestine. The Pale Horse was making itself known, and it was becoming more apparent with every passing day that Hitler, Mussolini, and the Middle East nations were not happy about the outcome of WWI and that it was all getting ready to blow up in the faces of Europe, Russia, Great Britain, and America.

Reoccupying the territories that Germany lost in WWI was Hitler's first objective, so in 1937 he invaded France, Belgium, the Netherlands, and Denmark. Once again, the rider of the Red Horse of Germanic warriors set out on a ride to take peace from the earth. Hirohito withdrew from a stalemate in northern China and began advancing to the lands of the South Sea for the resources he needed, such as oil, coal, steel, and rubber. But in 1938, something happened that would change the course of the world, fulfill many Bible prophecies, and bring us to the brink of WWIII, where we are in January 2024, as I write this book.

While Mussolini stripped Jews of their citizenship in 1938 and then attempted to invade Greece and Hitler annexed Austria and invaded Czechoslovakia, American drillers discovered oil in Saudi Arabia. The Arabian American Oil Company (ARAMCO) was formed, and a pact was made to sell America cheap oil in exchange for military protection. "...And see thou hurt not the oil." The US set up a military base in Saudi Arabia and housing for them and their families along with staging areas and dwellings for the American oil companies who were allowed to drill and produce oil as WWII raged on. This agreement triggered fierce resentment among fundamentalist Muslims who felt that the Muslim country of Saudi Arabia should not enter agreements with infidels and especially not allow them to set up military bases and housing to live there. This was burning smoke in the nostrils of what used to be the White Horse of the Islamic Ottoman Empire. In the coming years, the agreement would be one of the sparks that ignites the Pale Horse into action and a major contributing factor that propels the Black Horse into becoming the next world power. Meanwhile, Russia's Stalin and Germany's Hitler were hatching a plan.

The next year, Russia's Stalin agreed to fund Hitler's invasion of Poland in exchange for East Poland, so Hitler invaded Poland. Stalin wanted East Poland because every past invasion of Russia had come through Poland. Meanwhile, Japan's Hirohito invaded Mongolia, Siberia, and the Dutch East Indies. France and Great Britain declared war on Germany in response to the Poland invasion, but their attempt to attack ended in failure.

Fueled by a string of victories, Hitler targeted France the following year. America launched an embargo against Japan, and the rest of its allies soon followed suit. This infuriated Hirohito, and he felt his new strategy in the South Sea was threatened by America's military base in Hawaii called Pearl Harbor. The following year, in 1941, Roosevelt proceeded to add insult to injury and froze all of Japan's US assets. Hitler hatched a plan to betray Stalin after he conquered Poland. Instead of sharing Poland with Stalin like they had agreed, he invaded Stalin's Russia. This was a fatal mistake that would motivate Stalin to join forces with Great Britain and America against Hitler's reign of bloodshed.

Hitler launched Operation Barbarossa on June 22, 1941, and invaded Russia. Stalin felt so betrayed by Hitler's invasion of Russia that he hid in his chambers for weeks in a comatose state, unable to respond. He had an agreement with Hitler to divide Poland between them, and he had funded Hitler's war against it. Hitler continued to advance his troops and annihilate Russia while Stalin remained dazed and unable to respond to the situation. After weeks of losses, Stalin's generals finally overcame their fear and entered his chambers to admonish him of the dire situation. Stalin snapped out of his daze and launched a counteroffensive that was largely unsuccessful until Russia's greatest ally showed up in late 1942—winter. Russia was well-equipped to fight in winter while Germany was not. Russian armies finally drove Hitler out of Russia, ending the first of four fronts in WWII. While this conflict was taking place, America was attacked and formally entered the war.

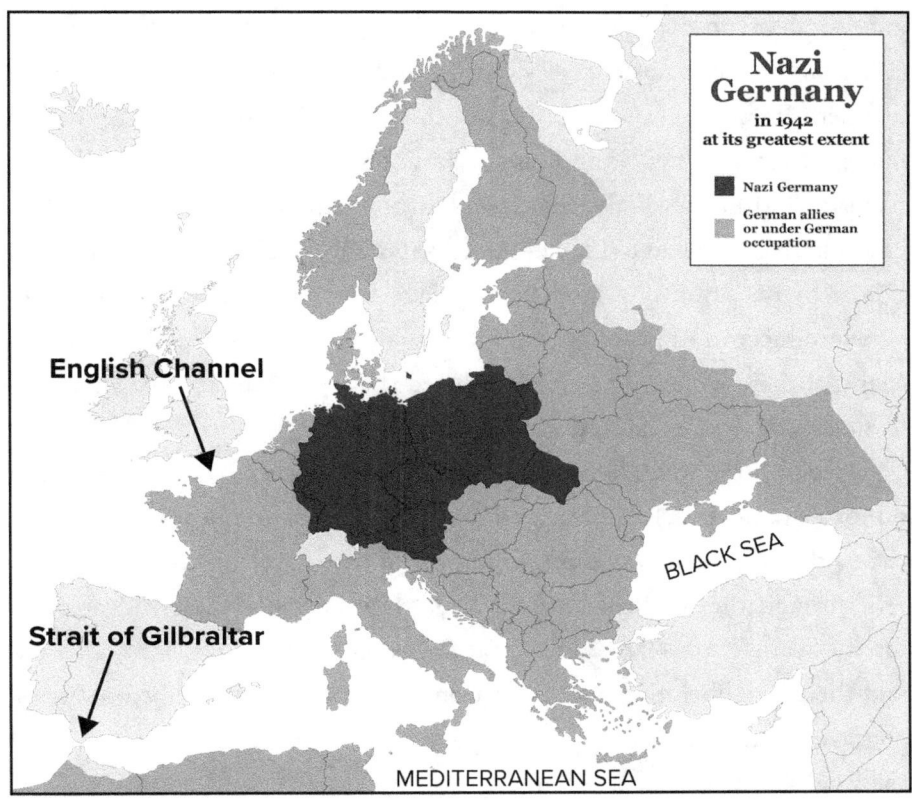

Nazi
Germany
in 1942
at its greatest extent

■ Nazi Germany

■ German allies
or under German
occupation

English Channel

Strait of Gilbraltar

BLACK SEA

MEDITERRANEAN SEA

Japan's attack still grieves the hearts of Americans. On December 7, 1941, Japan's Hirohito bombed Pearl Harbor in a surprise attack. The next day America declared war on Hirohito's Japan who, taking advantage of the chaos, invaded Hong Kong the same day. On December 11, four days after the Pearl Harbor attack, Germany, Italy, and Japan declared war on the United States. Great Britain and America knew they had to join forces to stop Hitler before dealing with Hirohito, so they took advantage of Hitler's betrayal and appealed to Stalin for help. In 1942, while Hirohito was invading Malaya in search of resources, Churchill, Stalin, and Roosevelt met and developed a strategy to defeat Hitler in a plan they called "Operation Torch."

To win the war against Hitler, Operation Torch had to secure shipping and the ability for naval vessels to travel through the Mediterranean Strait of Gibraltar, between Spain and Morocco, and the English Channel between northern France and the UK. Oh say, can you sea? This meant they had to liberate Morocco, the world's largest wine producer of that day, to be able to reach and liberate Italy, the second largest wine producer, from Hitler's control. They also had to liberate Algeria and Tunisia along Africa's northern border by the Strait of Gibraltar and liberate northern France, another top wine producer in the world, from Hitler's control over the English Channel. Many of these wine producers had started the resistance groups against Hitler's occupation of their countries.

To defeat the Red Horseman, first, America would need plenty of cheap oil for its naval vessels, and second, they would need to liberate and protect the world's top wine producing countries to ensure passage of its naval vessels through the Mediterranean. "...See thou hurt not the oil (protection for the world's top oil producer, Saudi Arabia, in exchange for cheap oil) and the wine (liberation and protection for the world's top wine producing countries that ensure safe passage into and through the Mediterranean and the English Channel)."

After liberating the countries that secured these passages, they set their sights on Italy, Mussolini's home base. The citizens of Italy had already voted Mussolini out of office and imprisoned him, but Hitler had rescued him and put him in charge of the Italian Social Republic. After liberating Italy from Hitler, Mussolini was caught trying to flee the country and then publicly executed as he hung upside down, ending the second of four fronts in WWII.

Alliances were now formed between the Black Horse and its rider and all the world's major wine producing countries of the Mediterranean along with the greatest oil producer of the Middle East, Saudi Arabia, leaving Hitler in shock.

On April 30, 1945, Hitler allegedly committed suicide by swallowing cyanide then shooting himself in the head. Seven days later, on May 7, an unconditional surrender was signed by Germany. Hitler had spent his entire childhood being shamed by his father and failing Germany was not a shame that he could endure after working so hard to prove his value as a human being. The third of four fronts in WWII had officially ended. Meanwhile, the rest of the world was busy putting America on an economic pedestal that stemmed from its oil deal with Saudi Arabia and its military might that had led to victory against Hitler.

In July 1944, forty-four nations met and unanimously made the US Dollar the World Reserve Currency in the Bretton-Woods Agreement along with forming the United Nations. "...I heard a voice in the midst of the four beasts say, 'A measure of wheat for a penny and three measures of barley for a penny.'" With Hitler out of the way, America could now deal with the last front of WWII, the lone mustang—Japan's Hirohito. Unfortunately, Roosevelt would not live to see his vision for America fulfilled and exact the vengeance that Americans so desperately wanted on Japan for Pearl Harbor. The stress of polio, the Great Depression, the Dust Bowl, Pearl Harbor, and WWII had taken their toll on Roosevelt, culminating in a sharp decline in his health. He died of a brain aneurysm during negotiations with Stalin, on April 12, 1945, shortly after the start of his fourth term in office.

The riders of both the Red and Black Horses had not only mounted their horses during the same year but had also died within two weeks of each other. America went into deep mourning and uncertainty. FDR was the man who represented a savior and father figure to them. He was all that they had known for twelve years and had turned their poverty into prosperity, redeemed their deaths into a new life, turned their fears into courage, and their hopelessness into hope. Was Harry Truman capable of exacting the vengeance the American people demanded against Japan for the attack on Pearl Harbor and ensuring the same path of prosperity and security that FDR had provided?

On August 6 of that same year, Harry S. Truman unleashed the atomic bomb that FDR had paved the way for in the Tennessee Valley on Hiroshima followed by the dropping of another atomic bomb on Nagasaki three days later. Hirohito finally surrendered. The fourth and final front of World War II was now defeated, officially ending WWII.

Unofficially, while most of the world was licking their wounds, the unforeseen fifth front was about to manifest and is still playing out today in 2024. The Middle East had not found their closure with the outcome of WWI either. They were disgruntled not only with Great Britain for carving up their Ottoman Empire into countries but also with Saudi Arabia for allowing infidels to occupy Muslim territory and graze in their pastures. But the UN was getting ready to put yet another burr under the saddle of the future Pale Horse that would escalate the situation leading to the October 7, 2023, attack on Israel by Hamas, the elected leaders of Palestine.

Darkness comes
and also light
one left weak
one gains might
White is down
Red is out
Black hits turbo
Pale én route

/

Additional Sources

"Benito Mussolini: The Father of Fascism: Evolution of Evil: Timeline." You-Tube, July 28, 2022. https://youtu.be/M0ltQn6AMGA?si=k42GIzw tp8XKCShL.

"Birth of a Führer: The Rise and Fall of Adolf Hitler: The Life of Adolf Hitler: Timeline." YouTube, March 18, 2023. https://youtu.be/pLFjw0zKcgQ ?si=MyIoUYReZ9hgWZFn.

Cole, Katherine. "Sparkling Wine in Wartime." SevenFifty Daily, February 10, 2020. https://daily.sevenfifty.com/sparkling-wine-in-wartime/.

"FDR Dies Amidst WWII Negotiations: FDR." YouTube, June 4, 2023. https://youtu.be/9o2E2XiPPXg?si=_Q_xQ1Ax438HUjE8.

"FDR Signs the Tennessee Valley Authority Act." YouTube, May 18, 2017. https://youtu.be/0AfVbBL02fM?si=P_Bi1uCP-UtMxD8R.

"The Great Palestinian Revolt 1936-1939: CHC." YouTube, January 14, 2022. https://youtu.be/hUZezmZyOtw?si=VmS4_6VNuZ219bsR.

"How FDR Revived the American Dream after the Great Depression: Impossible Peace: Timeline." YouTube, July 30, 2020. https://youtu.be/An0zm PRaOtc?si=OtkIQkOe6pG6RiXd.

Meloni, Giulia, and Johan Swinnen. "Algeria, Morocco, and Tunisia (Chapter 16) - Wine Globalization." Cambridge Core, February 2, 2018. https://www.cambridge.org/core/books/abs/wine-globalization/algeria -morocco-and-tunisia/23CD9BAB25F20569E2D10C9E008E4359.

"Operation Barbarossa: The Invasion That Doomed Nazi Germany: How the Nazis Lost: War Stories." YouTube, July 9, 2023. https://youtu.be/ZLty Dk118i4?si=oMrfAkNFFosa4sGy.

"The French Resistance: How Vintners Fought to Save Their Wine."

Spiral Cellars, April 12, 2023. https://www.spiralcellars.co.uk/stories/how-vintners-fought-to-save-their-wine/.

"The Reason Japan Attacked Pearl Harbor." YouTube, November 10, 2021. https://youtu.be/so4v_2zq35k?si=3tu1algTmz59EpEr.

"Stalin: The Man Who Had 7,000,000 of His Own People Killed: Evolution of Evil: Timeline." YouTube, July 5, 2022. https://youtu.be/tDBV5_AfqbE?si=oZd181qwaPsQBlfz.

United States Holocaust Memorial Museum, Washington, DC. "Operation Torch: The Anglo-American Invasion of French North Africa." United States holocaust memorial museum, January 7, 2019. https://encyclopedia.ushmm.org/content/en/article/operation-torch-algeria-morocco-campaign#:~:text=The%20Operation,concluded%20on%20November%2016%2C%201942.

"Why World Peace Failed after WWI: Total War: Timeline." YouTube, February 28, 2021. https://youtu.be/bd8bS6yGOXI?si=IxADNfbYI2tzBS1X.

"World War 2 Explained: Best WW2 Documentary: Part 2." YouTube, August 1, 2021. https://youtu.be/dq1_N0GLutw?si=K_OKojLh96zPE1K3.

"World War 2 Explained: Best WW2 Documentary: Part 2." YouTube, August 1, 2021. https://youtu.be/dq1_N0GLutw?si=K_OKojLh96zPE1K3.

Notes

ALLAH

THE BRINGER OF "DEATH"

THE "DESTROYER"

Hamas • Hezbollah • Houthis
Al-Qaeda • ISIS • Boko Haram
Taliban • Al-Fatah • Al-Shabab

Chapter 9

Won Thing Leads to Another

And when he had opened the fourth seal,

I looked and behold a pale horse:

1)…and his name that sat on him was Death,

2) and hell followed with him

3) And power was given unto them over a fourth part of the earth,

4) to kill with sword, and with hunger, and with death, and

with the beasts of the earth.

Revelation 6:7–8

Allah has ninety-nine names that characterize him, one of which is the Bringer of Death or the Destroyer. "…and his name that sat on him was death." Since the fall of the Ottoman Empire after WWI, Muslims have been divided by the borders of their countries with no central leader to fight for their cause of reestablishing a caliphate. This has caused multitudes of revolutions, uprisings, and terror groups ("liberators/freedom fighters") to arise and fight in the name of Allah alone with the Quran as their anchor and spirit guide. The problem is the Quran has over twenty versions, and they all disagree. Their battle cry is "Allahu Akbar," or Allah is Greater(est).

Because the caliphate no longer has a central leader, the rider of this horse isn't a physical human being. It is Allah, Bringer of Death. These terror groups will break out in four major waves and are the hell that will follow the Pale Horse in gruesome acts of Jihad that force submission to Sharia law. They have been in a form of perdition, so to speak, but are about to start breaking out of it and give birth to the Pale Horse. They also attack any enemies that hinder them from doing that, by any means necessary. This unholy trinity will be the next entity rising to world power, and we will likely see it in our lifetimes. In this series, you will see that this is not only prophesied in the Book of Revelation, but also Daniel and other prophets along with Jesus himself in the Gospels.

When the White Horse of the Ottoman Empire was in power, it did not force conversion to Islam or Sharia law. Non-Muslims were allowed to practice their faith or no faith at all; they just had to do things like pay higher taxes. There were sects of Muslims, under the Ottoman Empire (the powerless Pale Horse), who remained disgruntled with the sultans for this reason. This sect of Muslims is known as fundamentalists. They strictly adhere to the teachings of Muhammad and insist on the implementation of strict Sharia law over every human being in the world as the one and only goal of Islam.

Their stated goal today is to reestablish a caliphate that is under strict Sharia law, through the Pale Horse's various forms of Jihad, by any means necessary. Their first target for a caliphate is the Middle East. This requires the removal of the nation of Israel, which sits in the middle of their former and future caliphate. Once they achieve that goal and become the next world power, they will force the entire world, country by country to submit to Sharia law. Mosques used to display a crescent moon on top representing total subversion of the Middle East, but now they display a full moon representing global domination. It's ironic that Muslims proclaim that Jesus was a prophet but don't apply his prophecies to themselves.

...yea, the time cometh that whosoever killeth you (Christians and Jews) will think that he doeth God a service. — Jesus

John 16:2

This attempt for domination is already taking place at a staggering rate in the Middle East, Africa, Southeast Asia, and other countries. Since WWII, 21% or 42 of the 195 countries in the world have either come under some form of Sharia law or have Sharia law courts that allow it to be practiced. Those forty-two countries contain 41.49% of the world population, as you will see in the next chapter. "…And power was given them (the horsemen, its rider and the hell that follows it) over a fourth part of the earth."

It should be noted that not all Muslims claim to want this and consider this sect of Muslims to be in the pale and not representative of the mainstream Muslim religion. But, with over twenty versions of the Quran that all disagree with each other and no original writings to fall back on, it is difficult to establish what Muslims actually believe.

For now, let's continue our journey and pick up where we left off. WWII has ended, and while most of the world is letting out a sigh of relief, tensions continue to escalate in the Middle East as the UN places yet another burr under the saddle of the Pale Horse.

The UN passed Resolution 181 on November 29, 1947, forming two additional states from the already carved-up Ottoman Empire—one for Israel and one for Palestine. Saudi Arabia and other Middle East nations rejected the resolution because it recognized Israel as a state in what was once strictly Muslim territory under the White Horseman of the Ottoman Empire. Before his death, Franklin D. Roosevelt had assured Saudi Arabia that he would not vote in favor of this UN resolution, but he wasn't around anymore. Truman, feigning to be none the wiser, voted in favor of it.

On May 14, 1948, David Ben-Gurion became the first prime minister of Israel, and in one day, Israel became a nation. Jews began returning to their homeland from all over the world, sparking a massive revival in America because Bible prophecy was being fulfilled before their eyes. But while America basked in the glory of the revived nation of Israel and great prosperity, five Middle East nations marched to war against Israel.

Who hath heard such a thing?
Shall the earth be made to bring forth in one day?
Or shall a nation be born at once?
For as soon as Zion travailed, she brought forth her children.
Isaiah 66:8

Therefore, behold, the days come, declares the Lord,
that it shall no more be said, The Lord liveth
who brought up the children of Israel out of the land of Egypt,
but, The Lord liveth who brought up the children of Israel
from the land of the north,
and from all the lands whither he had driven them:
And I will bring them again into their land that I gave unto their fathers.
Jeremiah 16:14–15

Immediately after this resolution passed, an attack was launched on Tel Aviv followed by an all-out attack on Israel by Egypt, who led Saudi Arabian forces, Syria, Lebanon, and Iraq. The next year, the war ended with Gaza and the West Bank under Jordanian and Egyptian control along with Israel gaining more Arab territory. The Arabs in Palestine were left feeling that Israel couldn't be defeated and that they needed to take matters into their own hands but had no resources to do so. But all that was about to change in the second Arab-Israeli war.

Another Arab-Israeli war broke out in 1956 when the Suez Canal Crisis escalated to the invasion of Egypt by Great Britain, France, and Israel. With the US and the UN backing Egypt, they were forced to withdraw, and Egypt became emboldened to begin aiding rebel groups seeking independence from British occupation in the Middle East. Many guerrilla groups began forming and attacking Israel. Syrian groups attacked Israel from the Golan Heights and groups from Lebanon and Jordan also launched attacks. This escalated to the third Arab-Israeli war, and after Israel defeated the countries involved in this war, the first of four waves of terror groups began to formally emerge as a model for the rest of the Middle East.

On June 5, 1967, the third Arab-Israeli war, known as the Six Day War, broke out with the United Arab Republic (Egypt, Syria, Jordan, Iraq, and Lebanon) attacking Israel. The war ended with Israel obtaining more Arab territory which included the Golan Heights from Syria, more of the West Bank along with East Jerusalem from Jordan, and the Gaza Strip and Sinai Peninsula from Egypt. This is where the Middle East realized they could not defeat Israel in a conventional war, and it spawned the formation of the second of four waves of terror groups to formally emerge as the hell that follows the Pale Horse of Jihad. In 1967 the Marxist group called The Palestinian Liberation Organization (PLO) formed with Syria as its key supporter. From the PLO a branch sprouted called the Popular Front for the Liberation of Palestine (PFLP) and their General Command (PFLP-GC). Terror attacks began taking place across the world. The first model of a terror attack for these groups to follow happened during the 1972 Munich Olympics, sponsored by Russia. While the Pale Horse was gasping for air from the smoke in its nostrils of Israel becoming a nation and the defeat from several wars against it, the smoke of another fire went up their nostrils.

In 1973, the US and Saudi Arabia, once the anchor of Islam, created the Petro Dollar. The Petro Dollar required all oil purchased from Saudi Arabia to be paid for with US dollars. This agreement not only made the United States dollar increase in value and the royal Saudi family filthy rich, but also caused fundamentalist Muslims and terror groups to seethe in anger against both countries. Saudi Arabia had allowed the Black Horse to plant both of its hind hooves of military and money in their pasture.

Capitalism was now the scourge of the Middle East among Islamic fundamentalists, including Osama Bin Laden. He made it no secret that he was a staunch opposer of this corruption, but before he could cause any real problems for the royal family, two things happened that created a third wave of terror groups to formally emerge and follow the Pale Horse of Jihad in its conquest of global domination. In 1979, Russia invaded Afghanistan, and the Islamic Revolution kicked off in Iran.

Iran was a continuation of the kingdom of Persia and had retained absolute power since 1501 BC throughout all the clashes of the Middle East. Note that this empire existed since 4000 BC. Persian power was periodically interrupted by various empire changes, but they managed to remain partially or fully in control of their base for nearly six thousand years, from 4000 BC to AD 1979. This is, by far, the most important sentence to highlight concerning the books that follow in this series.

Moving on, in 1979 a Muslim revolution toppled the secular Persian Shah of Iran. The Shah had made it impossible for the vast Muslim population to adhere to the Quran by making it illegal to wear the hijab (women's head scarf) and for men to have facial hair, except for the mustache. After the Muslim revolution, the Shah was exiled and replaced by the Ayatollah Ruhollah Musavi Khomeini. It seems the Pale Horse had found a base and was about to drive Persia out of Iran. This is where non-Muslim leaders of countries learned that when you keep Muslims from practicing their faith, your government is at risk of being replaced by their own government in a violent revolution—if the Muslim population constitutes a number that can be considered a threat.

After Muslims took over Iran, a massive exodus happened along with the exile of the Persian hierarchy. The Persian kingdom was ushered out, and the New Islamic Order was ushered in. Iran had now become a base and grazing pasture for the Pale Horse. Iran began funding terror groups and are currently known as a state sponsor for global terrorism. They back many terror groups worldwide, three of which are Hamas in the Gaza Strip, Hezbollah in Lebanon, and the Houthis in Yemen.

While the free world was sanctioning Iran to weaken its new Muslim powerbase and fuel was skyrocketing while being rationed in the US, Jordan's future ISIS leader Abu Musab Al-Zarqawi and Osama Bin Laden, future leader of Al-Qaeda, left for Afghanistan to help fight the Russian invasion. Eleven years later in 1990, Muslims finally drove the Russians out of Afghanistan. Shortly after that, an extremist group, known as the Taliban, took over the Afghani government.

So far, Iran and Afghanistan have been taken over by Islamic fundamentalists. As of 2023, Iran represents 1.11% of the world population and Afghanistan represents .53%. The prophecy of the Pale Horse says he gets power over 25% of the world and these two countries represent 1.64% of it. Terror groups have now built-up momentum, but a fourth wave of terror groups are about to formally emerge after violent uprisings in the Middle East and Africa.

From 2010 through 2011, protests broke out starting in Tunisia and Egypt and then spreading to other Middle East nations, toppling some of their authoritarian government dictators. These uprisings created a void that ISIS quickly filled from 2013 to 2015 in Libya and Syria, but they also attacked Iraq. This is where we all learned that their acts of violence fulfilled all the ways that the hell following the Pale Horse would manifest. They beheaded, killed, raped, plundered, and ravaged these countries and then, toward the close of their three-and-a-half-year reign of terror, they began feeding their soldiers alive to dogs as a new form of punishment. "...And power was given unto them to kill with sword, and with hunger, and with death, and with the beasts of the earth." The Arab Spring spawned another wave of terror groups, inspired by the successes of these uprisings and ISIS. And this is how we arrived at where we are today from the time of Rome when John received that amazing and mysterious prophecy on the island of Patmos to now.

It all started with the rise and reign of the White Horse and will end with the reign of the Pale Horse that will become (or maybe is, depending on when you read this book) the next world power. This is why Jesus warned his

Church that the end of all things would be ushered in by the White Horse of Revelation and would end with the Pale Horse of Revelation.

Now that we know the who, what, when, how and why, let's find out exactly where that one-fourth of the world that the Pale Horse has power over stands today. In doing so, we will begin to understand why it seems that the world has descended into madness. The Pale Horse is dangerously close to achieving power over one-fourth of the earth and maybe even has exceeded it, depending on what perspective you take.

>...who is able to make war with it? (Islamic terror cell groups)
>Revelation 13:4

Stop them! stop them!
If you dare
now their roots
are everywhere
hell breaks out
in the east
Who can stop
this rising beast?

Additional Sources

"99 Names of Allah (God)." IslamiCity. Accessed January 8, 2024. https://www.islamicity.org/covers/99-names-of-allah/index.php?c=20.Alphabetical-List&referer=menu.

Afary, Janet. "Iranian Revolution." Encyclopaedia Britannica, June 23, 2009. https://www.britannica.com/event/Iranian-Revolution.

"Arab Spring." Encyclopaedia Britannica, September 7, 2011. https://www.britannica.com/event/Arab-Spring.

"The Arab-Israeli War of 1948." U.S. Department of State, Office of Historian, Foreign Service Institute, . Accessed January 11, 2024. https://history.state.gov/milestones/1945-1952/arab-israeli-war#:~:text=The%20Arab%2DIsraeli%20War%20of%201948%20broke%20out%20when%20five,Israel%20on%20May%2014%2C%201948. (According to the website, "Milestones in the History of U.S. Foreign Relations" is no longer maintained.)

"Investigating Islam with Dr. Jay Smith (2 Corinthians 10:5)." YouTube, September 15, 2023. https://youtu.be/40DclW84HkM?si=qaOISX2x3rhtlXBc.

"Osama Bin Laden Biography: The World's Most Wanted Man." YouTube, November 25, 2017. https://youtu.be/20bkbHpqf8s?si=NgiiK37OLKTeouBQ.

"The Soviet Invasion of Afghanistan and the U.S. Response, 1978–1980." Office of the Historian. Accessed February 2, 2024. https://history.state.gov/milestones/1977-1980/soviet-invasion-afghanistan#:~:text=At%20the%20end%20of%20December,large%20portions%20of%20the%20country.

"Total Immigration to Israel by Year (1948-Present)." Jewish Virtual Library. Accessed January 11, 2024. https://www.jewishvirtuallibrary.org /total-immigration-to-israel-by-year.

"United Nations Resolution 181." Encyclopaedia Britannica, July 29, 2011. https://www.britannica.com/topic/United-Nations-Resolution-181.

Notes

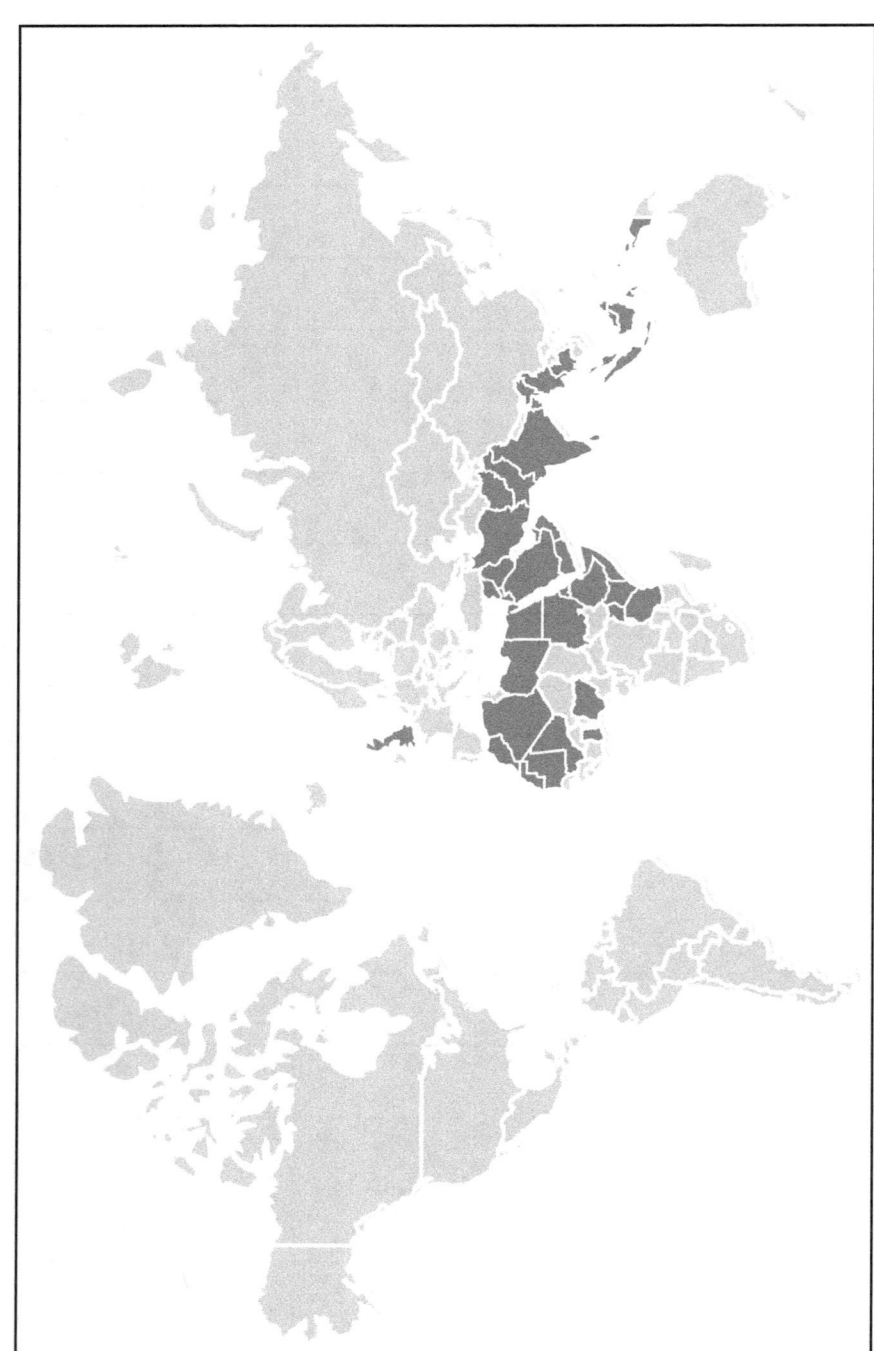

The dark shaded countries practice some form of Sharia law.

Chapter 10

In "The Pale"

This might seem like a boring, mundane, and overwhelming chapter, but it is one of the most important chapters, demanding the complete focus of every reader. Because of this, you might want to set this book aside until you have a day off to read it and have a highlighter in hand when you do. You will not see the full scope of these current events unless you fully understand how all these boring statistics are about to drastically impact your country, your life, and the lives of your children. And you will not know to apply them to the prophecy of the Pale Horse or how to impactfully and tactfully share with others why our world seems to be in such chaos.

The world is in the process of transitioning from the United States being the world power to Islam becoming the next world power. The world just hasn't realized it yet, and maybe our governments are in denial. In 2015, it was estimated that by the year 2050 the Muslim Population of the world was expected to rise by 73% while the Christian Population is only expected to rise by 35%. Bear in mind, that doesn't include the massive loss of Christians being slaughtered worldwide by extremist groups and governments. It also doesn't include the explosion of Muslim converts taking place over the last two decades.

The difference between Christians and Muslims is that Muslims now control over 25% of the world, in a governing sense of the word, and Christians control 0%. In addition to that, Islamic nations line the entire Mediterranean Sea along the coast of Africa and could easily take control of the Mediterranean Strait, just as the Houthis in Yemen took control of the Red Sea Strait in 2024. Christian persecution in the twentieth century far outweighs their persecution in the previous nineteen centuries combined. In the US, the FBI has labeled Christians as the biggest terrorist threat while overseas. The world is literally morphing into the early phases of an Islamic Caliphate unnoticed by most Christians because they are watching Europe for the emergence of the Antichrist.

There appears to be a pattern or progression that has played out since 1979 based on an explosion in the population growth of Muslims and terror groups worldwide. Muslims can have as many wives as they want and produce staggering numbers of children while most of the rest of the world encourages and funds abortions, limits the number of children that can be born, or promotes birthrates of one to two children per woman.

> In that day, saith the Lord, I will smite every
> HORSE with astonishment, and his RIDER with madness
> and will open my eyes upon the house of Judah (Israel), and
> will smite every horse of the people with blindness.
> Zechariah 12:4

Here is the progression that seems to have the world in constant upheaval, wondering why our governments seem to have gone mad and their citizens seem to be blind to what is going on:

First, extremist terror groups set up bases in countries with high Muslim populations. Second, as the Muslim population increases, laws begin to change in stages or all at once to a moderate or mixed form of Sharia law that allows non-Muslims to be under a separate court and Muslims to be under an Islamic court based on Sharia law. Third, when the Muslim population grows larger than other populations or terror groups take over, Sharia law is implemented over everyone through various means. Fourth, masses of people seek refuge in other countries as they flee the atrocities that take place when strict Sharia law is instituted. These refugees include non-Muslims, honest Muslims, but also devious Muslims associated with terror groups having malintent. Fifth and last, strict Sharia law is implemented on everyone, and more refugees flee from those countries into surrounding countries, increasing the Muslim population of surrounding countries in a second wave of refugees. Then the process repeats itself in the surrounding countries where people fled to as the Muslim population increases in those countries. The terrorists can't be vetted because no one is able to discern them from anyone else. "Who is able to make war with it?" Sometimes it happens all at once when a country gets a new leader.

So, let's look at what this progression has recently accomplished in Africa first and then the Middle East. Finally, we will look beyond the Pale into other parts of the world where this progression is playing out and add them all together to see how much of the world is already under some form of Sharia law as this Pale Horse and the hell that follows it morphs before our eyes into the next world power. The figures on the following pages are based on 2023 and 2024 statistics.

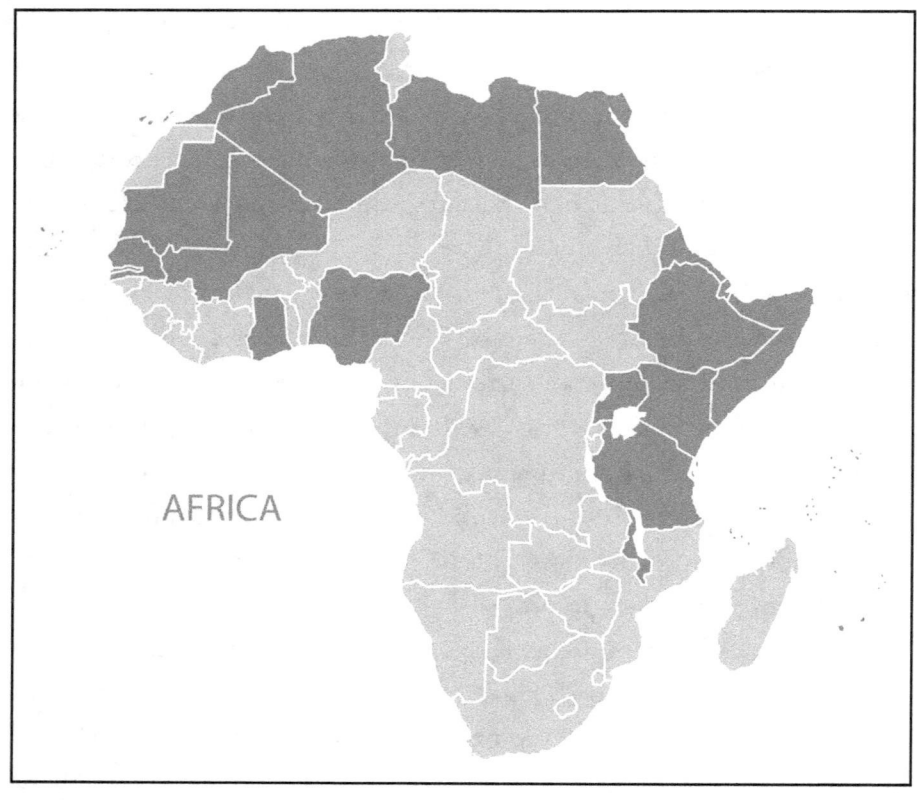

AFRICA

AFRICA

All citizens of the following countries in Africa are under Sharia law with varying degrees of brutal and inhumane punishment. The year that Sharia law was implemented is also listed to show how most of this has happened in our lifetime.

Country	Year	% of world population
Algeria	1984	.57%
Comoros	2018	.01%

Egypt	1980	1.4%
Ethiopia	1995	1.57%
Gambia	2015	.03%
Indonesia	2002	3.45%
Libya	1973	.09%
Malawi*	now	.26%
Mali	2012	.29%
Mauritania	2012	.06%
Morocco	1956	.47%
Nigeria**	1999	approx 1%
Senegal***	unknown	.22%
Somalia	2009	.23%
Sudan (Northern)	1983	.6%

Total % of world population in Africa under strict Sharia law = 10.25%

** Malawi's leaders are in process of implementing Sharia law as of March 2024.

** Twelve of 36 states in Nigeria practice Sharia law. Boko Haram and other groups have killed 62,000 Christians in Nigeria so far (as of March 2024) as they seek to make Nigeria an Islamic state. As of January 2023, they control the northern third of Nigeria equaling approximately 1%. If we were to see the carnage, it would resemble the same carnage we witnessed when ISIS took over Syria, Libya, and Iraq.

*** Records are not accessible in some countries.

Of the countries listed in the previous chart, Sudan, Nigeria, and Somalia practice female genital mutilation and use severe forms of punishment for breaking Sharia law that include cutting off limbs, thrashings, and stoning. Indonesia practices female genital mutilation, stoning, and thrashings. Mauritania and Mali practice female genital mutilation and stoning. Libya practices thrashings. Gambia, Ethiopia, Egypt, Kenya, and Tanzania practice female genital mutilation.

All the following countries in Africa practice Sharia law for Muslims only, but remember, it is a progression.

Country	Year	% of world population
Eretria	1991	.05%
Kenya	unknown	.68%
Tanzania	1971	.84%
Uganda	unknown	.6%

Total % of world population in Africa
with only the Muslim population under Sharia law = 2.17%

The following countries in Africa have Sharia laws that apply only to things like marriage, divorce, family law, etc., or mixed laws that accommodate common and Sharia law along with other forms of law. They are in early phases of the progression.

Country	Year	% of world population
Ghana	1992	.42%
Djibouti	1992	.1%

Total % of world population with mixed laws, some Sharia laws = .52%

Total % of world population in Africa under some form of Sharia law is…
12.94%

We haven't even gotten to the Middle East yet and are over halfway to the one-fourth of the earth that the Pale Horse and the hell that follows it are given power over in the Pale Horse prophecy. Terror groups are rampant in Africa and are slowly moving further south, taking it over country by country. Southern Africa is inhabited by mostly Christians, so there is a band of killing and conflict that stretches all the way across Africa between the Christians and Muslim countries. As the Muslim population grows, they push their way further south and take over the Christian territories one at a time. The most recent example of this is the killing of Christians taking place in Nigeria by Boko Haram and other terror groups. This group is similar to what we saw with ISIS, but we aren't hearing as much about it. Other countries that have Muslim populations are asking for Sharia law, and they could fold overnight, like Niger where over 90% of the population wants Sharia law.

Now let's look at the Middle East, where all of this started.

THE MIDDLE EAST

All the citizens in the following countries in the Middle East are under Sharia law with varying degrees of brutal and inhumane punishment.

Country	Year	% of world population
Saudi Arabia	1992	.46%
Iran	1979	1.11%
Gaza/West Bank	2002	unknown
Yemen	1992	.43%
Bahrain	2002	.02%
Qatar	2004	.03%
Iraq	1995	.57%
UAE	1971	.12%

Total % of world population in the Middle East
under strict Sharia law = 2.05%
Plus, the West Bank and Gaza

Of the Middle East countries listed above, Iran and Yemen practice limb removal, thrashings, stoning, and female genital mutilation. Saudi Arabia

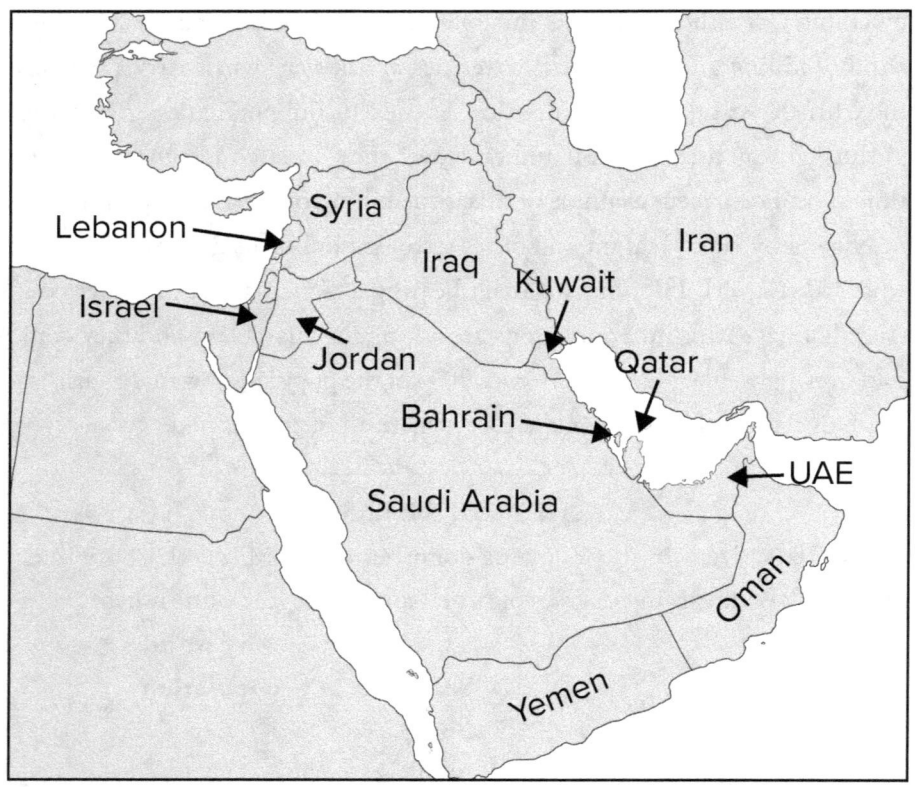

and the UAE practice limb removal, thrashings, and stoning. Saudi Arabia also practices beheadings and sometimes in mass. Qatar practices limb removal and stoning. Iraq practices stoning and female genital mutilation.

The following Middle East country applies Sharia law to Muslims only.

Country	Year	% of world population
Oman	1991	.06%

Total % of world population in Africa
with only the Muslim population under Sharia law = .06%

All the following countries in the Middle East have mixed laws, some of which are Sharia law and apply only in certain cases, like civic law, etc. It should be noted that especially in countries like Syria the government looks the other way or is unaware of the citizens and innumerable terror groups that commit atrocities worse than what the law of their country allows in every category.

Country	Year	% of world population
Syria	1973	.29%
Israel (West Bank/Gaza)	mixed	.11%
Lebanon	1989	.07%
Jordan	unknown	.14%
Kuwait	1991	.05%

Total % of world population with mixed laws, some Sharia laws = .66%

Total % of world population in the Middle East
under some form of Sharia law...
2.77%

If we add the percent of the world population in Africa under some form of Sharia law to the Middle East countries that are under some form of Sharia law, we get **15.71%**. Remember, the purpose of many terror groups is to first bring the entire Middle East under one caliphate where strict Sharia law is enforced and all forms of corporal punishment are executed. Once the Middle East is under one caliphate, the progression moves to Israel and America, followed by the rest of the world.

So far, as it stands in January 2024, in Africa and the Middle East, the Pale Horse and the hell that follows it is stomping over 15.71% of the 25% that is prophesied in the Book of Revelation. Now, let's travel beyond the

Pale into surrounding countries, where Sharia law has spread in its many forms of progression, to find out exactly what percent of the world population is subject to some form of Sharia law as of 2024. Brace yourself, because when we add it to the list, the total is shocking.

OTHER COUNTRIES

The following countries around the Middle East and stretching across Southeast Asia are under strict Sharia law with varying degrees of brutal and inhumane punishment.

Country	Year	% of world population
Afghanistan	1979	.53%
Brunei	2014	.01%
Malaysia	1997	.43%
Maldives	1997	.01%

Total % of world population outside of the Middle East and Africa under Sharia law = .98%

Of the above countries, Brunei practices limb removal and thrashings. Afghanistan practices stoning. Malaysia practices stoning and female genital mutilation. Maldives practices thrashings. We all know that Afghanistan is filled with terror groups and far worse things happen in the pale of that country along with others. These countries have territories that are far beyond the reach of the leaders to stop abuses because there are no or few roads or any way to reach or call authorities. The same is true for many areas included in this chapter. In many areas, it is a free-for-all of Sharia anarchy and terror groups.

The following countries outside of Africa and the Middle East and stretching across Southeast Asia are under Sharia law that applies to Muslims only. This is where things get a little shocking.

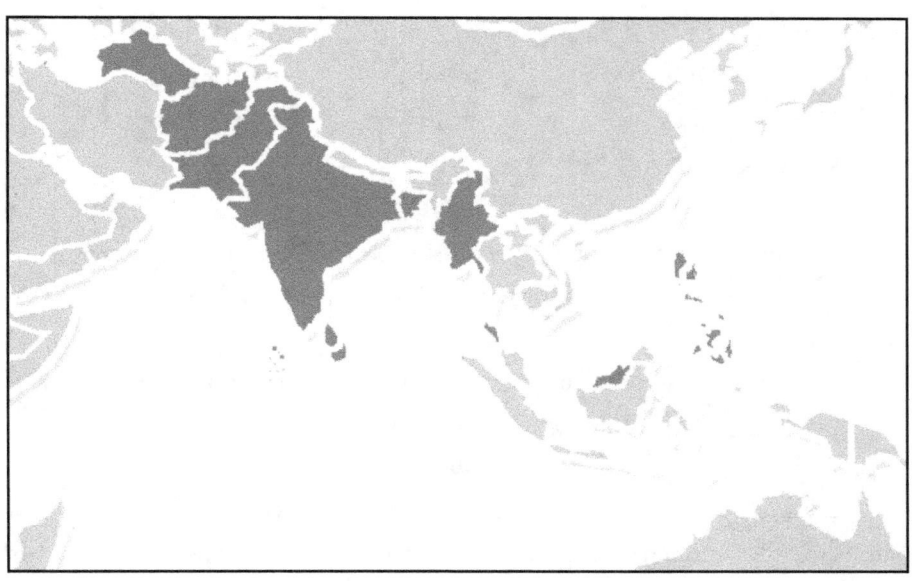

Country	Year	% of world population
The Philippines	1977	1.46%
Myanmar	1988	.68%
India	1937	17.76%
Bangladesh	1937	2.15%
Sri Lanka	unknown	.27%

Total % of world population outside Middle East and Africa
where only Muslims are under Sharia law = 22.32%

The following countries outside of Africa and the Middle East have laws that are mixed where some are Sharia, some are not, or various situations are different, like only civil law or marriage/divorce, etc.

Country	Year	% of world population
Pakistan	2010	2.99%
Turkmenistan	1991	.08%

Total % of world population outside of Middle East and Africa
where Sharia laws are mixed with others = 3.07%.

Total world population outside of Middle East and Africa
under some form of Sharia law is...
26.37%

Let's add all the countries from every part of the world together and find out exactly how much of the world is under strict Sharia law, has only Muslims under Sharia law, and/or has mixed laws with Sharia law.

% of the world population where...
- the country is under Sharia law   13.28%
- only Muslims are under Sharia law   24.55%
- Sharia law is mixed with others and applied   3.66%

Total % of world population under some form of Sharia law or allows it
41.49%

T

This total means almost half of the world population is under some form of or allows Sharia law!!! But some places, like London, are not included in these statistics where Sharia law courts are allowed to operate.

You can see here how Sharia law is bleeding out beyond the Middle East and Africa into the rest of the world at a higher rate than strict Sharia law is taking over the Middle East and Africa. Extremely dense populations of Muslims live in northern India today, but they have also been scattered around the rest of the world due to refugees fleeing the hostilities of countries that practice strict Sharia law. Many places that aren't even mentioned here, like London, also have and allow Sharia law courts to practice.

But what does this all mean in relation to the prophecy?

That is really for you to decide for yourself and why we need to watch this development closely. You can monitor it and begin shading in the areas on the maps in this book as it continues to progress.

Here are my thoughts concerning these statistics: We can see that terror groups are allowed to practice in at least 25% of the world as the hell that follows the Pale Horse because little effort is made to stop them, partially because it is hard, if not impossible to do so. "...And power was 'given' them over a fourth part of the earth...'who is able to make war with it?'" I am of a school of thought that when 25% of the world population is completely subject to strict Sharia law with the strictest penalties, the Pale Horse and the hell that follows it will have already or will soon become the next world power and replace America. If you look at the maps, the regions where they have the strongest footing control vital waterways and straits...Oh say, can you sea?

The question is not what can we do about it but what must we do about it? Before we answer that question, let's review what we have learned and look at the implications of everything taking place a little closer.

Nations align

While others collide

a storm approaches

nowhere to hide

voices trumpet

behind every hill

a faint voice cries

stay in your peace and be still

Additional Sources

"Arab Spring." Encyclodaedia Britannica, September 7, 2011. https://www.britannica.com/event/Arab-Spring.

"Countries That Follow Sharia Law." The Business Standard, September 3, 2021. https://www.tbsnews.net/world/countries-follow-sharia-law-297286.

Jawad, Ashar. "25 Countries Where Muslim Population Will Increase the Most by 2050." Yahoo! Finance, November 18, 2023. https://finance.yahoo.com/news/25-countries-where-muslim-population-013430609.html.

"Sharia Law Countries 2024." World Population Review, n.d. https://worldpopulationreview.com/country-rankings/sharia-law-countries.

Chapter 11

The Some of all Things

Mark 37:13 — "And what I say unto you I say unto all, Watch."-Jesus

On this amazing journey, we learned the meaning behind each of the four horsemen and how the prophecies in the Book of Revelation revolve around power over the straits in the Mediterranean Sea. We have watched as each dominant world power or empire, from the time of Rome until now, was in decline while the next empire grew in strength until it became the next world power. All these events dovetailed into and out of each other leading us to where we are in 2024. The characteristics of all these world powers that have risen since the time of Rome match the characteristics of the Four Horsemen. The oil-based Black Horse of America is in rapid decline while countries under Sharia law and terror organizations are rapidly growing in numbers and gaining more control over the lifelines of the Red and Mediterranean seas. So, based on what we have watched take place, three things are for certain, and a fourth certainty is guaranteed in John's prophecy.

First, countries controlled by fundamentalist Muslims will unite and reestablish a caliphate before becoming the next world power. Second, as a result, America will cease to be the greatest world power. Third, militant Islamic groups will directly, indirectly, or both, cause the fall of America.

Fourth, the Pale Horse of Jihad is the last horsemen mentioned in Revelation, so it will be the last world power to arise. (The next book in this series will cover this extensively and line it up with the prophecies in Daniel.) But what happens after that? What can we expect?

So far, the first five seals have been opened and/or are in progress. The Roman Empire was in power when John received this mysterious and apocalyptic prophecy leading to the end of the world as we know it. Here's a condensed timeline of everything we covered so far:

- AD 70 — Rome is the world power and John receives the vision/ prophecy of the Four Horsemen.
- AD 286 — Rome is divided into east and west creating the Byzantine Empire and marking the beginning of the end of Rome.
- AD 536 — Sun is darkened by volcanic eruption, Dark Ages, prophetic sign.
    * Overlap between the Roman and Ottoman empires *
- Rome is weakened while the Ottoman Empire rises
- AD 570 — Muhammad is born, Islam spreads via holy wars, caliphate emerges.
- AD 1258 — Osman Gazi, heir to the throne and father of the next empire, is born as the son of the king of the Muslim Kayi tribe, who were expert warriors at shooting a short bow on horseback. "…And he that sat on him had a bow."

1ST SEAL OPENED

Rider with bow on White Horse
Global conquest on the back of the religion of Islam

- AD 1281 — Osman Gazi becomes the king of the Kayi Tribe when his father dies. "…And a crown was given him." Known as "Warrior of the Islamic Faith." "…And I saw, and behold a white horse."

- Osman Gazi, using a bow, defeats approaching Mongol Army, drives back crusaders. "…He that sat on him had a bow…and he went forth conquering." He then set his sights on defeating Rome "…and to conquer."
- AD 1453 — The Roman (Byzantine) Empire officially dies when the tenth Sultan, one of Osman Gazi's descendants, defeats the capital of the Byzantine Empire.

* Official birth of the Ottoman Empire *

2ND SEAL OPENED

Rider with sword on Red Horse takes peace from the earth
Global conquest through war on the back of Germanic warriors

- AD 1859 — Kaiser Wilhelm II born
- AD 1888 — Kaiser Wilhelm becomes Emperor of Germany, mounts Red Horse of Germany, greatest military power of that time
- AD 1889 — Hitler is born
- AD 1914 — WWI begins as Wilhelm backs Austria Hungary
- AD 1914 — Ottoman Empire/White Horse and rider align with Germany
- AD 1917 — Rising Black Horse of America declares war on Germany, ending WWI
- AD 1918 — WWI officially ends. White Horse down; territory is divided into Middle East nations.
- AD 1929 — Stock Market crash launches the Great Depression
- AD 1933 — Hitler comes to power, mounting Red Horse of Germany

3RD SEAL OPENED

Rider with scales on Black Horse
"measure of wheat/ 3 measures of barley for a penny,
see thou hurt not the oil and the wine."
Global conquest on the back of oil and capitalism

- AD 1930 — The Great Depression and Dust Bowl create severe conditions for America
- AD 1933 — Franklin D. Roosevelt becomes President of the United States of America and mounts the Black Horse.
- AD 1937 — Hitler, on back of Red Horse, starts WWI.
- AD 1941 — America enters war.
- AD 1942 — WWII ends. America becomes known as the greatest military power, now protecting oil of Saudi Arabia and wine-producing countries that line the Mediterranean and its straits. "…And see thou hurt not the oil and the wine."
- AD 1944 — The US dollar becomes the World Reserve Currency "…and I heard a voice in the midst…a measure of wheat for a penny and three measures of barley for a penny."
- AD 1973 — The Petro Dollar is born. All oil must now be purchased with the US dollar. The Black Horse and all future riders now have Global Domination, militarily and monetarily.

4TH SEAL OPENED

Pale Horse with rider named Death given power over ¼ of the earth
followed by hell
Global conquest of fundamental Islamic Muslim terror groups
to reestablish the Ottoman Caliphate that is under strict Sharia law,
followed by forcing the world to submit to it through terror and jihad
as the hell that follows the Pale Horse and his rider named Death (Allah,
Bringer of Death)

(See Chapter 10 for characteristics and fulfillment (too many to list here))

5ᵀᴴ SEAL OPENED

Souls taken by the Pale Horse and the hell that follows it
are under the altar of God crying out for vengeance and
are told to rest for a season until their brethren
are killed as they were...
This is in progress now.

6ᵀᴴ SEAL

"And I beheld when he had opened the sixth seal, and,
lo, there was a great earthquake; and the sun became
black as a sackcloth of hair,
And the moon became as blood;
And the stars of heaven fell unto the earth,
even as a fig tree casteth her untimely figs,
when she is shaken of a mighty wind.
And the heaven departed as a scroll when it is rolled together;
and every mountain and island were moved out of their places."
Revelation 6:12–17

Imagine the scene described in this verse about the sixth seal that can now suddenly unfold without warning if we do not watch. Maybe you believe that we will all be raptured out of this, but I would contend that we aren't going anywhere until we fulfill the Great Commission, and we haven't done that yet. If you were to tell your teenager to "Go clean your room and then we will go out to dinner," would you let him go to dinner before he was done cleaning his room? Probably not. We must reexamine what Paul told us about the rapture and accept the possibility that we might be here until the seventh trumpet sounds, like Paul told us.

7ᵀᴴ SEAL

When the seventh seal is opened, the seven angels with trumpets prepare to sound. After the seven trumpets finish sounding, the vials of God's wrath are poured out. We only know two things for certain:

- we aren't appointed to be here during that wrath, and
- we will meet the Lord in the air at the sounding of the last trumpet. The rest is speculation.

For God hath not appointed us to wrath…
1 Thessalonians 5:9

For the Lord himself shall descend from heaven with a shout,
with the voice of the archangel and with the trump(et) of God:
and the dead in Christ shall rise first: Then "WE" which are alive
and remain shall be caught up together with them in the clouds,
to meet the Lord in the air: and so shall we ever be with the Lord.
1 Thessalonians 4: 16–17

In a moment, in the twinkling of an eye,
AT THE LAST TRUMP(ET): for "the trumpet shall sound,"
the dead shall be raised incorruptible, and "WE" shall be changed.
1 Corinthians 15:52

Notice that Paul uses the word *we* in those verses. He expected to be a part of it and to still be here when the seventh trumpet sounded. By comparison, he did not say those of us who are ready will be raptured out of everything before the seventh trumpet sounds and those of you who remain will meet the Lord in the air at the sounding of the seventh trumpet. If Paul expected to still be here when the seventh trumpet sounded, why do we think we should expect anything different?

AMERICA

The "handwriting is on the wall." We already see America's rapid decline while terror groups rise in numbers, territory, and power of influence. Saudi Arabia and other Muslim nations are abandoning the dollar and joining the gold-backed, Russia- and China-led financial organization known as BRICS (Brazil, Russia, India, China, and South Africa). As of January 2024, BRICS represented 45% of the world's population and countries owning over 25% of the world's oil. America, by comparison, has 2.1%. The Petro Dollar that made America so rich and powerful will soon cease to exist. The United Arab Emirates has already abandoned the Petro Dollar. As a result, the US dollar will soon cease to be the World Reserve Currency. The USA will experience hyperinflation because of trillions of US dollars no longer being needed by the world to purchase their oil. Is the use of digital currency being planned because America and Europe know that this is inevitable? While America focuses on Russia and China and pressures Israel to cease their operations in Gaza, they ignore the real threat.

Over ten million illegal immigrants, who could be terrorists, are invading our southern border. Even if we close our southern border, they can gain entry through our northern border. Over twenty-two Islamic guerrilla communes (training camps) are in America and on the FBI watch list. Why are our leaders allowing this and will these illegal immigrants be joining those compounds and/or creating others? (See the source articles for this chapter.) In addition, Jihad against America has been called for by Iran due to the US backing of Israel in the Israel-Hamas war that started on October 7, 2023. During this war, US shipping was attacked by Yemen's Houthi rebels and had to be diverted from the Red Sea Strait of Bab-el-Mandeb to travel all the way around Africa, driving up our prices and hurting our already staggering economy. The entire world economy depends on entry to this strait, and now Hamas has shown the world that they control it. God forbid that terrorist groups also seize the strait that controls the Mediterranean.

THE WORLD ECONOMIC FORUM

It is almost a certainty that we will see cash eliminated in the US along with other countries in the northern hemisphere to survive the rapid BRICS take-over of the world economy and the crash of the dollar. The World Economic Forum (WEF) may gain control over America and Europe, even parts of the Middle East, but ultimately the terror groups will either infiltrate and overtake them or destroy them. They won't submit to a chip or any control outside of Islam. Is the WEF an extension of Germany? Is the Red Horse of Germany trying for a third round of global domination through the WEF? (Please watch the video source link on this.)

GERMANY

Germany played a large role in the fall of the Roman Empire and a major role in the fall of the Ottoman Empire. They caused the rider of the White Horse and their own Red Horsemen to fall off their horses during WWI and WWII along with causing both wars! So, with tensions escalating toward WWIII, we need to watch them closely and ask ourselves if their actions will play a role in causing the Black Horse of America to fall? As of January 2024, their militarily has become very active in response to Russia's invasion of Ukraine. They are ripe for a dictatorial government to arise during 2024 as their farmers refuse to farm and are protesting and opposing the government in the streets. Is Germany the lost tribe of Dan?

Dan shall be a serpent by the way, an adder in the path,
that biteth the horse heels, so that his rider shall fall backwards.
Genesis 49:17

RUSSIA AND CHINA

While Russia focuses on Ukraine and China focuses on Taiwan, neither one of them see the real threat. While they build up BRICS and look to Muslim countries to join in a silent war against the US dollar, they don't realize that they will be feeding the beast that will ultimately control the entire world, including them. If the US, Russia, China, and Europe didn't see each other as a threat, they could join against the real threat and not only back but join Israel in its never-ending wars against Iranian-backed terror groups. Russia and China will likely gain great power temporarily, like Great Britain did after WWI, but Russia and China aren't part of the four horsemen. Likely, they will be dragged into a war by a rope of alliances (that somehow starts with Germany again) to appease their new Muslim friends in their efforts to become the next world power thru BRICS. After all, in January 2024, they learned first-hand what happens to your economy with shipping if you don't back Muslim nations opposing Israel. He who controls the sea, controls the world. Just a reminder of something else that we have learned on our journey—All the countries on the coast of North Africa are Muslim countries and could easily make a choke point on the Mediterranean Sea in addition to the one that the Houthis made on the Red Sea in 2024. Oh say, can you sea?

EUROPE

Europe is already in dire straits because of an energy crisis after natural gas from Russia was cut off. When Russia invaded Ukraine, Europe imposed sanctions on Russia to weaken its economy, and Russia responded by cutting off Europe's supply of natural gas. Almost 45% of Europe's gas came from Russia, leaving its citizens unable to pay for the higher gas prices.

Has the day of Jacob's trouble already begun? Are America and Europe descendants of Jacob? Many believe they are. If so, as Muslims gain more power, the day of Jacob's trouble will continue to escalate. After all, this is truly a struggle between Jacob and Esau, and the Bible tells us the details of that struggle and how it will turn out in Genesis and Jeremiah.

For thus saith the Lord;
We have heard a voice of trembling, of fear and not peace.
Jeremiah 30:5

Alas! For that day is great, so that none is like it:
it is even the time of Jacobs trouble; but he shall be saved out of it.
Jeremiah 30:7

ISRAEL, GAZA, EGYPT, AND THE RED SEA CANAL(S)

Israel is known as the hallway of the world. Situated on the eastern Mediterranean seaboard, surrounded on every side by Muslim countries, it provides safe ports for shipping between all other countries and the countries of the Middle East. But years ago, the United States and Israel planned another canal that may soon be built to bypass Egypt's canal to the Mediterranean. This project is called the Ben Gurion Canal. (Read the source link by Richard Medhurst about the Ben Gurion Canal. Otherwise, you will not understand why certain elements in Israel may have chosen to overlook or hide the many warnings they received before the Hamas attack of October 7, 2023.) God promised Abraham that the descendants of Isaac would possess the gates of their enemies and that has never been more true than it is right now in 2024.

...and thy seed shall possess the gate of his enemies.
Genesis 22:17

In addition to the canal, The Temple Institute in Israel recently discovered a huge gold mine. They plan to use this gold to coat the third temple. There is no doubt that the Middle East countries and Russia are going to want that gold for BRICS. Israel has also recently discovered numerous natural gas reserves in the Mediterranean and are planning to run a pipeline through the Mediterranean Sea to Europe. This would alleviate the suffering that Russia has inflicted on Europe after cutting off their natural gas supply. Russia has numerous reasons to back Hamas, Hezbollah, and the Houthis against Israel and let them do their dirty work for them.

Israel was and is feeling more than fear from terror attacks in 2024 though. Many of their imports come through the Red Sea, which was blocked in 2024 by Yemen's Houthi rebels. Israel doesn't produce their own weapons, and now many of their weapons must travel all the way around Africa along with everything else they import, creating a huge impact on Israel's already failing economy. God forbid that the Muslim nation of Morocco be taken over by or join terror groups and block the Strait of Gibraltar, the only other entrance to the Mediterranean Sea—but it's likely coming.

These two straits, once giving Israel the advantage over its enemies, are now in danger of cutting them off from provisions and weapons. Israel could still get supplies from Europe, through the Mediterranean, if Turkey and Greece don't join the blockade. But it's very likely that at some point, they will. Oh say, can you sea? It is going to be a long and treacherous ride for everyone involved. Maybe you hold a view that you don't have to worry about any of this because the Church will be raptured out of it, but we are all still here.

THE GREAT TRIBULATION

The Great Tribulation is mentioned in the book of Revelation for the first time when the seventh seal is opened. The multitude around the throne when the sixth seal is opened had just come out of it, not through a rapture but the same way the people under the altar came out of it during the ride of the Pale Horseman. Everything that happens after that is in addition to and part of great tribulation and what I believe to be the Hour of Temptation that will come upon everyone dwelling on the face of the Earth. Submit to Islam to survive, be killed, or flee and go into hiding, and America is the last bastion of freedom from it.

Because thou hast kept the word of my patience,

I also will keep thee from the hour of temptation, which shall come upon
all the world, to try them that dwell on the earth.

Revelation 3:10

Countries, people, families, and cultures have all gone through tribu-
lation(s) in their comings and goings, risings and fallings. Be assured, "the
Great Tribulation" has begun and will continue to grow in territory and be
harder to endure as time progresses. Certainly, the Christians of Syria, Iraq,
and Libya were in great tribulation during the ISIS reign of terror, and they
weren't raptured out of it. The Christians in South Africa are certainly in
great tribulation as Boko Haram and other terror groups slaughter them little
by little. Israel is absolutely in great tribulation right now, February 2024, as
they fight these terror groups surrounding them on every side.

Be of good cheer, our redemption draweth nigh, and there is a very simple way we can bring this madness and chaos to an end. It is in our power
to stop it within the next ten years, but we must run at top speed and pour
everything we have into it before the doors close. It's time to bear down and
push because the length and duration of this process depends solely on us
and our determination to fulfill the Great Commission.

"Walk while ye have the light, lest darkness come upon you:..." — Jesus

John 12:35

Darkness comes

as does LAST Age

hope now shines

turning this page

one way through

for you and me

a path to end

all things we now see

Additional Sources

"BRICS Portal." BRICS Russia UFA 2015, n.d. https://infobrics.org/.

"BRICS: What Is the Group and Which Countries Have Joined?" BBC News, February 1, 2024. https://www.bbc.com/news/world-66525474#.

"Eastern Mediterranean (EastMed) Pipeline Project, Israel." NS Energy, n.d. https://www.nsenergybusiness.com/projects/eastern -mediterranean-pipeline-project/#.

"Farmers in Romania, France and Germany Continue Road Convoy Protests." euronews, January 21, 2024. https://www.euronews.com/2024/01/21/ farmers-in-romania-france-and-germany-continue-road-convoy-protests.

Fox, Tsivya. "Billions of Dollars of Gold Discovered under Eilat Mountains to Be Used to Rebuild Third Jewish Temple." Israel365 News, June 15, 2015. https://www.israel365news.com/298849/temple-mount -activists-find-billions-dollars-gold-jerusalem/.

"Germany Is Preparing for Possible NATO-Russia War." YouTube, January 16, 2024. https://youtu.be/i2qclzJJDMY?si=ONW9fcH-FecFcmJE.

Grollnek, Chris. "FBI's List of Terrorist Camps in America." Chris Grollnek, Active Shooter Expert | Keynote Speaker, May 9, 2020. https://www .chrisgrollnek.com/fbis-list-of-terrorist-camps-in-america/.

"Iran's IRGC Urges 'jihad' amid Gaza War." Iran International, November 2, 2023. https://www.iranintl.com/en/202311020708.

Keating, Joshua. "How a Yemeni Rebel Group Is Creating Chaos in the Global Economy." Vox, December 21, 2023. https://www.vox.com/world -politics/24010092/houthis-red-sea-shipping-yemen-israel-gaza.

Medhurst, Richard. "'Israel Destroys Gaza to Control World's Most Important Shipping Lane (Part II)." Al Mayadeen English, December 1, 2023.

https://english.almayadeen.net/articles/analysis/-israel--destroys-gaza-to
-control-world-s-most-important-shi.

Scharf, Avi. "All Ships Attacked by Yemen's Houthis in the Red Sea."
Haaretz.com, January 15, 2024. https://www.haaretz.com/israel-news
/security-aviation/2024-01-15/ty-article-magazine/30-attacks-all-red
-sea-ships-targeted-by-the-houthis/0000018c-5df7-d6f9-afbc-5df
f7a430000#.

"The World Economic Forum." World Economic Forum, n.d. https://www
.weforum.org/.

"Wrap up: Biden Administration's Policies Have Fueled Worst Border Crisis in U.S. History." United States House Committee on Oversight and
Accountability, January 18, 2024. https://oversight.house.gov/release
/wrap-up-biden-administrations-policies-have-fueled-worst-border
-crisis-in-u-s-history%EF%BF%BC/.

Zeniewski, Peter, Gergely Molnar, and Paul Hugues. "Europe's Energy
Crisis: What Factors Drove the Record Fall in Natural Gas Demand
in 2022? – Analysis." IEA, March 14, 2023. https://www.iea.org
/commentaries/europe-s-energy-crisis-what-factors-drove-the-record
-fall-in-natural-gas-demand-in-2022#.

Map of the countries who practice some form of Sharia law. Compare this map to the one on the next page.

The rectangle indicates the 10/40 Window. Note the similarity to the previous map where Sharia law is practiced.

Chapter 12

A Brief Enter-Mission

How can we bring the madness and chaos to an end? Jesus told us this will end when we share the gospel with every creature and publish it in every nation. Have we done that yet? No. Do you honestly think God is going to rapture his Church out of this chaos before we complete the Great Commission Jesus gave us?

> And this gospel of the kingdom shall be preached in all the world
> for a witness unto all nations: and then shall theend come." — Jesus
> Matthew 24:14

By comparison, he did not say, and this gospel of the kingdom shall be preached to as many nations as you can until the rapture. As a matter of fact, if you look at the maps to your left, most of the unreached are in the 10/40 Window where Sharia law is being implemented and where terror groups flourish. So how long is this going to take? How can we accomplish this?

According to a spokesperson from Christian Aid, a group that funds missionaries, we are ten years away from reaching everyone in the 10/40 Window, as of 2023. So, we could fulfill the Great Commission in our lifetime, and perhaps much sooner if we buckle down, but much longer if we fail to act aggressively. Many giants in the land are threatening to close the door of opportunity we have right now to complete that mission. We might not be able to defeat those giants by facing them directly, but we can certainly beat them to the finish line if we act quickly and do it wholeheartedly.

As many of you know, a digital currency is in the works in much of the world as the dollar fails against Russia and China's BRICS alliances. When this digital currency is implemented, the government could disallow funding to Christian organizations. The FBI has already asked banks in America to flag all donations to former President Donald Trump, churches, and Christian organizations along with any Bible purchases. The American economy is also in danger of crashing and never recovering. It is imperative that we provide mass support for all organizations that help fund missionaries while the window remains open.

Also, the giant of the WEF is trying to restrict our resources, make us eat bugs, and "own nothing and like it." This is their 2030 agenda, meaning they want to accomplish this by the year 2030. This is exactly three years prior to when Christian Aid projects can reach every nation with the gospel. The finish line is 2030, and we simply must beat WEF to it. As fate would have it, we have a rare opportunity to do that right now, but that opportunity could begin closing in 2024.

Many countries are experiencing a massive influx of immigrants fleeing the takeover of Sharia law in the 10/40 Window and the brutal terror groups trying to reestablish an Islamic caliphate. Others are immigrating to flee dire economic situations in South America. If or when Trump is re-elected as president, he has stated he will deport them immediately. Many of us are praying for God to send laborers into the harvest so we must ask ourselves if this situation is an answer to that prayer. Are these people coming over our borders the answer and our new mission into the 10/40 Window and South America? If we can reach them with the gospel and place their hands in the hand of any missionary funding organizations that could fund them before they are deported, they may eagerly choose to return from where they came to share the gospel. We can also pour funds into these organizations to sponsor other missionaries who are willing to go into these regions. (In the back of this book is a list of a few organizations that help fund missionaries.) But you can do something else—if you are not good at sharing face to face.

This book is designed to be not only a hook but a net to reach and gather Muslims, Christians, and anyone else it reaches. The series title is designed to invoke the curiosity of Muslims because of the mention of the caliphate and lead them to the understanding that, indeed, Jesus was a prophet, as they now believe him to be, along with informing them of the accuracy of his final prophecy. When they take the journey of reading this book, it might lead them to faith in the Bible and away from faith in the Quran. Personally, my first objective is to buy as many copies of this book as I can afford and place them at every church, mosque, and Jewish synagogue I can find locally and then mail it to as many others as I can in my state. I also hope to mail it to select politicians and everyone I know in Israel. Maybe you already know a Muslim who you can hand this book to. This book definitely has potential to lead them to Jesus and the Bible as the truth. There is an interesting story that I want to share to alleviate any doubts about the explosive impact that this strategy could have on the world—

In John 21 we read about how the future disciples of Jesus were fishing all day and caught nothing. Jesus told them to cast their nets off the other side of the boat, and when they did, they caught so many fish that it broke their nets. Maybe you have been trying to reach the people in your country with little or no success. Maybe it's time to cast your net off the other side of the boat into the unlikely waters. You only have to reach one person—if it is the right person. Then that person may have the opportunity to reach millions if they are in the right place at the right time. That time might be very soon.

If you want to follow the progress of the unreached, you can visit a site called The Joshua Project. They have a map posted of the 10/40 Window and all areas that remain unreached with the gospel. They can also connect you with a list of missionaries if there is a specific region you want to fund or sponsor.

Jesus told us when the end would come, and we simply can't leave the Great Commission for the next generation to complete because they might not be able to do it, and if they must do it, they might have to endure things beyond anything we would ever want to imagine or be able to comprehend.

Now our journey
comes to its end
will you go?
will you send?
shortly we will
launch again
gather your family
also your friend

...TO BE CONTINUED

And they sang the song of Moses
the servant of God, and the song of the Lamb, saying,
Great and marvelous are thy works, Lord God Almighty;
just and true are thy ways
thou King of saints
Who shall not fear thee, Oh Lord, and glorify thy name?
for thou only art holy:
For all nations shall come and worship before thee;
For thy judgements are made manifest.

REVELATION 15:3–4

Missionary Funding Organizations

To donate to Christian organizations
that financially support missionaries worldwide

Servants of Christ Intl
8406 18th Street Road
Greely, CO 80634-5128
970-939-5128
https://servantsintl.org/process-services/

Christian Aid Mission
1807 Seminole Trail
Suite 200
Charlottesville, VA 22901
434-977-5650
https://www.christianaid.org/

The Christian and Missionary Alliance
One Alliance Place
Reynoldsburg, OH 43068
380-208-6200
https://cmalliance.org/who-we-are/great-commission-fund/

About the Author

I grew up in the '60s and '70s before Asperger's and Autism became widely known, so like many, I went undiagnosed until I reached fifty-eight years old. Because of this, when my siblings, cousins, and peers wouldn't play with me, I developed a relationship with art and paper to pass the time. When visiting my grandmother, she often sat me at a table with a huge stack of paper, pencils, pens, and a spirograph while my cousins and siblings went outside or upstairs to play. As an adult, my talent in art slowly shifted to poetry where I vented my pain and frustration from constant rejection in jobs and various relationships. It was during my empty nest stage of life that I was finally able to focus on matters of my heart instead of revolving around everyone else's hearts.

I was raised in a Christian family. When I was twelve years old, our pastor preached a sermon mentioning that God considered the age of accountability to be twelve. Remember, I was twelve years old when I heard it. Spurred on by my fully cemented fear of rejection and going to hell, I went straight home and spent the next year reading the entire Bible from cover to cover, even the genealogies. At that age, I was so desperate for love that when I read the story of how Jacob had worked for Leban for much of his adult life in exchange for Rachel, who he loved with all of his heart, and then she died before they could spend their life together, I put my Bible down for weeks and cried every time I tried to pick it back up. I finally finished reading it before I turned thirteen.

I remember telling God several times that it wasn't fair for him to hold me accountable for things I couldn't understand that I had read about Bible prophecy and how unfairly he had treated Jacob. When I got to the New Testament and read about the voice of Rachel crying and how she couldn't be comforted, I went through another short season of grief, but my confusion about prophecy was at the forefront of my mind.

I had numerous conversations with my pastor at that time about what certain things in prophecy meant, but he didn't really give me concrete answers, so I set them aside and proceeded with my life until my children moved out. It was then that these questions resurfaced and became amplified when the World Trade Center was attacked in 2001 and ISIS surfaced in 2013. I returned to my best friend, paper, and filled thirty-seven notebooks with information about events, history, and prophecy that were later put onto tri-fold board time capsules and have now become a book.

As it turns out, my greatest disability in life, that caused me so much emotional trauma, has now become my greatest strength. As an Aspie, I have to have all my ducks in a row , all my belongings organized, and all my questions answered. And my relationship with God and paper will likely continue until I can no longer write because I know that neither one of them will ever reject or abandon me because they have always been my best and only friends. My gift has finally made room for me.

A man's gift maketh room for him,
and bringeth him before great men.
Proverbs 18:16

www.ingramcontent.com/pod-product-compliance
Lightning Source LLC
Chambersburg PA
CBHW060541130626
46553CB00002B/849